Messages

MESSAGES

A Book of Poems

Compiled by Naomi Lewis

faber and faber

LONDON · BOSTON

First published in 1985
by Faber and Faber Limited
3 Queen Square London WC1N 3AU

Filmset by Wilmaset Birkenhead Merseyside
Printed in Great Britain by
Redwood Burn Limited Trowbridge Wiltshire
All rights reserved

British Library Cataloguing in Publication Data

Messages
1. Children's poetry—English
I. Lewis, Naomi
821'.914'0809282   PR1195.C47
ISBN 0–571–13646–X
ISBN 0–571–13647–8 Pbk

Contents

'I TELL THE TALE THAT I HEARD TOLD'

ANGELS, DEMONS, PHANTOMS, DREAMS

THE WILD, THE TAMED

'COINS FOR THE FERRY'

'A HOST OF FURIOUS FANCIES'

'. . . YET WISH I WALKED WITH THEE'

'THE TREE OF MAN WAS NEVER QUIET'

DIFFICULT RELATIONS

YESTERDAY'S TOMORROW, TOMORROW'S YESTERDAY

Introduction

Several thoughts ran through the making of this book. One was that every good poem, however well known, is for someone, somewhere, a find – Eureka! – met for the first time. The second – a mystery but a fact – was that a good poem can be read again, any number of times, and still be a discovery. Countering this was the thought that too many anthologists casually lift the same poems from one book into another, without ever looking into the author's not-so-familiar works. And the fourth thought was that every day exciting new poems are written, many by poets not yet known at all, and that some of them should be here. They are. A number of new poems, some never before in anthologies, some never before in print, are in this book. So are some not too well-known poems by Traherne and Shelley and Hardy, Lawrence, Ted Hughes and Newbolt (yes), and other surprises too. And several major landmarks, that stand up to every change of fashion and climate, have, very rightly, a place.

What, though, *is* a good poem? Today there are no set rules for composing one, nor any limit to subject; but you still know when the whole thing doesn't work. Poems are made out of words, and a writer needs to be on the same terms with words as musicians are with their own particular instrument. This isn't a matter of rhyme and metre and scansion. Philip Larkin's *Days* is an instance of a perfect poem that doesn't use any of these techniques. But try setting it out as prose. Nor can you hope to reason away the *rightness* of the stunning image in the last two lines. Yet Larkin, like Auden, writes far more often in rhyming, metrical stanzas. It was a surprise to me to find how many modern poets in this book had chosen to use that intricate

[15]

form the sonnet. But they use it as a contemporary vehicle: see Lawrence Whistler's brilliant *Epitaph*. It's the content and the conversational voice that carry the form: the better the poet the more easily he uses – and hides – technique.

Less easy to track down is the poet's way of looking. Well, every reader of myths and fairy tales (or, if you like, of that potent tale by W. W. Jacobs *The Monkey's Paw*) knows about that very odd business of the wish. Three are given. The first two are so thoughtlessly used that the third has to be spent on repairing the damage. So the wisher ends (at best) rather bruised, where he or she began. It happens again and again. The missing ingredient is of course imagination. And because so many people never think to engage it in their lives, Wish Four, on the other side of the failures, still lies unchosen by all but a few. I count the writers of poetry among these few. They have, or should have, the kind of imagination that sees over to the other side of an experience: the region of Wish Four. Whatever the subject, light or serious, a game of marbles, a visit to a fortune-teller, a search for something lost, a death, it becomes a whole in the poem, and the reader at once perceives and shares this view. John Clare wrote of the very poor illiterate peasants of his village in the earlier nineteenth century that when personal tragedies struck them they seemed dumb and perplexed; but when they heard a tragic ballad they wept. A poem, you could say, is a personal message. It is meant for you.

Now to omissions, always the first line of critical complaint. But no one knows better than the conscientious compiler what is *not* in the book and why. Sometimes extreme length is the difficulty – *The Ancient Mariner*, say, which should be in the landscape (icescape or seascape) of everyone's mind. But it must be given entire. In poems where a part can carry the special character of the whole, a sizeable part has been given: of *Prothalamion*, *Verses on the*

Death of Doctor Swift, *The Masque of Anarchy*, *Thyrsis*, *Hiawatha*, *The Rubáiyát of Omar Khayyám*: some others too. *Lycidas*, happily, is given in full. You are surprised to find some of these here? Do not be. In their several ways they are all poems of peculiar power and interest, and this book is the right place to find them when the moment comes. But more recent poems, still in copyright, offer other resistances. The daunting obstacles in the way of permission (so often teasingly set up by 'Estate of . . .') have kept out several desired items. Brecht's extremely long and haunting poem *Children's Crusade 1939* is the most important casualty.

The arrangement is, more or less, by subject, not by date and time; so many poems, after all, are from this century. Still, yesterday's poets have some highly contemporary thoughts; Langland (fourteenth century) doesn't even know that he is voicing the enlightened modern refutation of that disastrous old Descartes. As for Swift . . . The subject lines get crossed, of course; a poem about a boy or a bird may also be about spring or night or death or dreams, or music, magic, ghosts. But if left for a bit it will usually choose its own section. And in particular groups within the larger ones – on angels, say (don't miss this winged assembly), or time – it is of extraordinary interest to see the unexpected ways in which different poets respond to these unpredictable themes. In another notable section, poets write about the problems and the pleasures of their craft, and a modern Greek, Cavafy, encourages a young beginner. Even the first step, he says, 'is a long way above the ordinary world.' Po Chü-i in Ancient China declaims his verse to the hills and sky but keeps away from men because they think him mad. But the most comprehensive statement comes from a writer aged nine. 'Poetry is poetry,' he begins.

It may be good
It may be bad
It may be happy
It may be sad . . .

It may rhyme
Like this
And be sublime
Like this
It may make sense
It may not
It may make pounds, shillings and pence
It may not.
A poet must have a good imagination
Like Shakespeare
He should have satisfaction from his creation.

Take it line by line – it could hardly be better put.

Finally a particular tribute of thanks and appreciation to my Faber editor Phyllis Hunt, not only as a miracle of patience and a bringer of order into chaos, but as an ally whose scholarship and imagination made her the best possible companion in this voyage of wonders and discoveries.

A Pen, a Paintbrush, a Guitar

The First Step

The young poet Evmenis
complained one day to Theocritos:
'I've been writing for two years now
and I've composed only one idyll.
It's my single completed work.
I see, sadly, that the ladder
of Poetry is tall, extremely tall;
and from this first step I'm standing on now
I'll never climb any higher.'
Theocritos retorted: 'Words like that
are improper, blasphemous.
Just to be on the first step
should make you happy and proud.
To have reached this point is no small achievement:
what you've done already is a wonderful thing.
Even this first step
is a long way above the ordinary world.
To stand on this step
you must be in your own right
a member of the city of ideas.
And it's a hard, unusual thing
to be enrolled as a citizen of that city.

Its councils are full of Legislators
no charlatan can fool.
To have reached this point is no small achievement:
what you've done already is a wonderful thing.'

C. P. CAVAFY

Poetry

Poetry is poetry
It may be good
It may be bad
It may be happy
It may be sad.

Some like poetry
Some detest it
Some write it beautifully
By now you must have guessed it.

It may rhyme
Like this
And may be sublime
Like this
It may make sense
It may not
It may make pounds, shillings and pence
It may not.
A poet must have a good imagination
Like Shakespeare
He should have satisfaction from his creation.

PETER (9)

[20]

Madly Singing in the Mountains

There is no one among men that has not a special failing:
And my failing consists of writing verses.
I have broken away from the thousand ties of life:
But this infirmity still remains behind.
Each time that I look at a fine landscape,
Each time that I meet a loved friend,
I raise my voice and recite a stanza of poetry
And I am glad as though a God had crossed my path.
Ever since the day I was banished to Hsün-yang
Half my time I have lived among the hills.
Often, when I have finished a new poem
Alone I climb the road to the Eastern Rock.
I lean my body on the banks of white stone:
I pull down with my hands a green cassia branch.
My mad singing startles the valleys and hills;
The apes and birds all come to peep.
Fearing to become a laughing stock to the world,
I choose a place that is unfrequented by men.

PO CHÜ-I
translated by Arthur Waley

Poems of Solitary Delights

What a delight it is
When on the bamboo matting
In my grass-thatched hut,
All on my own,
I make myself at ease.

[21]

What a delight it is
When, borrowing
Rare writings from a friend,
I open out
The first sheet.

What a delight it is
When, spreading paper,
I take my brush
And find my hand
Better than I thought.

What a delight it is
When, after a hundred days
Of racking my brains,
That verse that wouldn't come
Suddenly turns out well.

What a delight it is
When, of a morning,
I get up and go out
To find in full bloom a flower
That yesterday was not there.

What a delight it is
When, skimming through the pages
Of a book, I discover
A man written of there
Who is just like me.

What a delight it is
When everyone admits
It's a very difficult book,
And I understand it
With no trouble at all.

What a delight it is
When I blow away the ash,
To watch the crimson
Of the glowing fire
And hear the water boil.

What a delight it is
When a guest you cannot stand
Arrives, then says to you
'I'm afraid I can't stay long,'
And soon goes home.

What a delight it is
When I find a good brush,
Steep it hard in water,
Lick it on my tongue
And give it its first try.

TACHIBANA AKEMI
translated by Geoffrey Bownas
and Anthony Thwaite

Poetical Economy

What hours I spent of precious time,
   What pints of ink I used to waste,
Attempting to secure a rhyme
   To suit the public taste,
Until I found a simple plan
Which makes the lamest lyric scan!

When I've a syllable *de trop*,
    I cut it off, without apol.:
This verbal sacrifice, I know,
    May irritate the schol.;
But all must praise my dev'lish cunn.
Who realise that Time is Mon. ...

I gladly publish to the pop.
    A scheme of which I make no myst.,
And beg my fellow scribes to cop.
    This labour-saving syst.
I offer it to the consid.
Of ev'ry thoughtful individ. ...

If playwrights would be thus dimin.:
    The length of time each drama takes,
(*The Second Mrs Tanq.* by Pin.
    Or even *Ham.*, by Shakes.)
We would maintain a watchful att.
When at a Mat. on Wed. or Sat. ...

HARRY GRAHAM

Plaits

When I was small my mother did my hair
While I stood in the study, obedient,
Rehearsing foreign words encoded on the spines of books,
Taking a view of the landscaped room.
Its ornamental light dulled by real morning on
Firm hills of history and letters round me;
The favoured lake of recent books, piled and reflected by
  black marble;

Creeping art and green poetry growing with me up the
   walls.
I chanted titles off; she plaited down my hair;
Neatly tied up I'm launched upon the world.

*Dore   *Stoneware and Porcelain
Modigliani, Sacred   Imitations, Life Studies
Circles,   Wallace Stevens
Dore, Modigliani   Stoneware, Porcelain
Sacred Circles   Imitations, Life Studies
Monet at   Turner Sketches
Giverny   A Writer's Journal
Duckworth   Richard
Ortega y Gasset   Jefferies
Missing   Animals in Art
Persons   Arms and Armour
Dodds, Phaidon   Playing
Frozen Tombs   Cards
Tibetan Carpets   Unease and Angels
The Word as Image   The Word as Image

Now I plait my own hair
And it's a darker tone;
Daily scales fast; no shelved music;
I read my own books, silent and private;
Gravely I watch my self's reflected flicker past my face;
Late, every morning, I upbraid myself.

*These two plaits are meant to be read simultaneously by two voices.

TABITHA TUCKETT (14)

The First Thing to Do in a House

The first thing to do in a house
Is find the poet's pen,
Then feed God's mouse
And water Mary's hen.

ANNA WICKHAM

From In Memory of W. B. Yeats

... Earth, receive an honoured guest;
William Yeats is laid to rest:
Let the Irish vessel lie
Emptied of its poetry.

Time that is intolerant
Of the brave and innocent,
And indifferent in a week
To a beautiful physique,

Worships language and forgives
Everyone by whom it lives;
Pardons cowardice, conceit,
Lays its honours at their feet.

Time that with this strange excuse
Pardoned Kipling and his views,
And will pardon Paul Claudel,
Pardons him for writing well.

In the nightmare of the dark
All the dogs of Europe bark,
And the living nations wait,
Each sequestered in its hate;

Intellectual disgrace
Stares from every human face,
And the seas of pity lie
Locked and frozen in each eye.

Follow, poet, follow right
To the bottom of the night,
With your unconstraining voice
Still persuade us to rejoice;

With the farming of a verse
Make a vineyard of the curse,
Sing of human unsuccess
In a rapture of distress;

In the deserts of the heart
Let the healing fountain start,
In the prison of his days
Teach the free man how to praise.

W. H. AUDEN

The Long Small Room

The long small room that showed willows in the west
Narrowed up to the end the fireplace filled,
Although not wide. I liked it. No one guessed
What need or accident made them so build.

[27]

Only the moon, the mouse and the sparrow peeped
In from the ivy round the casement thick.
Of all they saw and heard there they shall keep
The tale for the old ivy and older brick.

When I look back I am like moon, sparrow, and mouse
That witnessed what they could never understand
Or alter or prevent in the dark house.
One thing remains the same – this my right hand

Crawling crab-like over the clean white page,
Resting awhile each morning on the pillow,
Then once more starting to crawl on towards age.
The hundred last leaves stream upon the willow.

EDWARD THOMAS

Sheep Meadow

French spoken
across the snow
on Sheep Meadow
evokes a very rich hour
of the Duke of Berry . . .
three men traversing
a field of snow –
one of them alone –
hedged by trees
on the south side
where the towers
of the city rise . . .
one of those hours

in early afternoon   ‑
when nothing happens
but time makes room

SAMUEL MENASHE

This poem was suggested by an illustration in the
illuminated manuscript *Les Très Riches Heures du Duc
de Berry*.

The Bystander

I am the one who looks the other way,
In any painting you may see me stand
Rapt at the sky, a bird, an angel's wing,
While others kneel, present the myrrh, receive
The benediction from the radiant hand.

I hold the horses while the knights dismount
And draw their swords to fight the battle out;
Or else in dim perspective you may see
My distant figure on the mountain road
When in the plains the hosts are put to rout.

I am the silly soul who looks too late,
The dullard dreaming, second from the right.
I hang upon the crowd, but do not mark
(Cap over eyes) the slaughtered Innocents,
Or Icarus, his downward-plunging flight.

Once in a Garden – back view only there –
How well the painter placed me, stroke on stroke,
Yet scarcely seen among the flowers and grass –
I heard a voice say, 'Eat,' and would have turned –
I often wonder who it was that spoke.

ROSEMARY DOBSON

To Jane

The keen stars were twinkling,
And the fair moon was rising among them,
    Dear Jane!
  The guitar was tinkling,
But the notes were not sweet till you sung them
    Again.

As the moon's soft splendour
O'er the faint cold starlight of Heaven
    Is thrown,
  So your voice most tender
To the strings without soul had then given
    Its own.

The stars will awaken,
Though the moon sleep a full hour later,
    To-night;
  No leaf will be shaken
Whilst the dews of your melody scatter
    Delight.

Though the sound overpowers,
Sing again, with your dear voice revealing
    A tone
Of some world far from ours,
Where music and moonlight and feeling
    Are one.

PERCY BYSSHE SHELLEY

Harp of Wild and Dream-like Strain

Harp of wild and dream-like strain,
When I touch thy strings,
Why dost thou repeat again
Long-forgotten things?

Harp, in other, earlier days,
I could sing to thee;
And not one of all my lays
Vexed my memory.

But now, if I awake a note
That gave me joy before,
Sounds of sorrow from thee float,
Changing evermore.

Yet, still steeped in memory's dyes,
They come sailing on,
Darkening all my summer skies,
Shutting out my sun.

EMILY BRONTË

Fife Tune

(6/8) for Sixth Platoon, 308th I.T.C.

One morning in spring
We marched from Devizes
All shapes and all sizes
Like beads on a string,
But yet with a swing
We trod the bluemetal
And full of high fettle
We started to sing.

She ran down the stair
A twelve-year-old darling
And laughing and calling
She tossed her bright hair;
Then silent to stare
At the men flowing past her –
There were all she could master
Adoring her there.

It's seldom I'll see
A sweeter or prettier;
I doubt we'll forget her
In two years or three.
And lucky he'll be
She takes for a lover
While we are far over
The treacherous sea.

JOHN MANIFOLD

A Toccata of Galuppi's

Oh, Galuppi, Baldassaro, this is very sad to find!
I can hardly misconceive you; it would prove me deaf and
　　blind;
But although I take your meaning, 'tis with such a heavy
　　mind!

Here you come with your old music, and here's all the good
　　it brings.
What, they lived once thus at Venice where the merchants
　　were the kings,
Where St. Mark's is, where the Doges used to wed the sea
　　with rings?

Ay, because the sea's the street there; and 'tis arched by . . .
　　what you call
. . .Shylock's bridge with houses on it, where they kept the
　　carnival:
I was never out of England – it's as if I saw it all!

Did young people take their pleasure when the sea was
　　warm in May?
Balls and masks begun at midnight, burning ever to
　　mid-day
When they made up fresh adventures for the morrow, do
　　you say?

Was a lady such a lady, cheeks so round and lips so red, –
On her neck the small face buoyant, like a bell-flower on its
　　bed,
O'er the breast's superb abundance where a man might
　　base his head?

Well, (and it was graceful of them) they'd break talk off and
  afford
– She, to bite her mask's black velvet, he, to finger on his
  sword,
While you sat and played Toccatas, stately at the
  clavichord?

What? Those lesser thirds so plaintive, sixths diminished,
  sigh on sigh,
Told them something? Those suspensions, those solutions
  – Must we die?
Those commiserating sevenths – 'Life might last! we can but
  try!'

'Were you happy?' – 'Yes.' – 'And are you still as happy?' –
'Yes. And you?'
– 'Then, more kisses!' – 'Did *I* stop them, when a million
  seemed so few?'
Hark! the dominant's persistence, till it must be answered
  to!

So an octave struck the answer. Oh, they praised you, I dare
  say!
'Brave Galuppi! that was music! good alike at grave and gay!
I can always leave off talking, when I hear a master play.'

Then they left you for their pleasure: till in due time, one by
  one,
Some with lives that came to nothing, some with deeds as
  well undone,
Death came tacitly and took them where they never see the
  sun.

But when I sit down to reason, think to take my stand nor
  swerve,
While I triumph o'er a secret wrung from nature's close
  reserve,
In you come with your cold music, till I creep thro' every
  nerve.

Yes, you, like a ghostly cricket, creaking where a house was
  burned –
'Dust and ashes, dead and done with, Venice spent what
  Venice earned!
The soul, doubtless, is immortal – where a soul can be
  discerned.

Yours for instance, you know physics, something of
  geology,
Mathematics are your pastime; souls shall rise in their
  degree;
Butterflies may dread extinction, – you'll not die, it cannot
  be.

As for Venice and its people, merely born to bloom and
  drop,
Here on earth they bore their fruitage, mirth and folly were
  the crop:
What of soul was left, I wonder, when the kissing had to
  stop?

Dust and ashes!' So you creak it, and I want the heart to
  scold.
Dear dead women, with such hair, too – what's become of
  all the gold
Used to hang and brush their bosoms? – I feel chilly and
  grown old.

ROBERT BROWNING

Children's Country

I am Called Childhood

I am called Childhood, in play is all my mind,
To cast a coyte,[1] a cockstele,[2] and a ball;
A top can I set, and drive in its kind;
But would to God these hateful bookes all
Were in a fire brent[3] to ponder small![4]
Then might I lead my life always in play,
Which life God send me to mine endying[5] day.

SIR THOMAS MORE

[1]quoit   [2]shuttlecock   [3]burnt   [4]small substance   [5]dying

Lullabies

Than mind a child
That yelps like this
The rice-field weeds
I hate so much
I'd rather gather.

Than mind a child
That yelps like this
I'd all day work
The loom that creaks
Noisy as crickets.

'Is she sound asleep?' –
This I asked the pillow.
The pillow said, 'Yes, yes,
She's fallen fast asleep.'

ANON
translated by Geoffrey Bownas
and Anthony Thwaite

The Wallpaper

When I was only five years old,
  My mother, who was soon to die,
Raised me with fingers soft and cold,
      On high;

Until, against the parlour wall,
  I reached a golden paper flower.
How proud was I, and ah! how tall,
      That hour!

'This shining tulip shall be yours,
  Your own, your very own,' she said;
The mark that made it mine endures
      In red.

I scarce could see it from the floor;
   I craned to touch the scarlet sign;
No gift so precious had before
           Been mine.

A paper tulip on a wall!
   A boon that ownership defied!
Yet this was dearer far than all
           Beside.

Real toys, real flowers that lavish love
   Had strewn before me, all and each
Grew pale beside this gift above
           My reach.

Ah! now that time has worked its will,
   And fooled my heart, and dazed my eyes,
Delusive tulips prove me still
           Unwise.

Still, still the eluding flower that glows
   Above the hands that yearn and clasp
Seems brighter than the genuine rose
           I grasp.

So has it been since I was born;
   So will it be until I die;
Stars, the best flowers of all, adorn
           The sky.

EDMUND GOSSE

My Youngest Daughter Getting Up in the Morning

She is like snow
fallen from the roof
when she rises;
the windows
in the room below
rattle

ADÈLE DAVIDE

The Hippopotamus's Birthday

He has opened all his parcels
    but the largest and the last;
His hopes are at their highest
    and his heart is beating fast.
O happy Hippopotamus,
    what lovely gift is here?
He cuts the string. The world stands still.
    A pair of boots appear!

O little Hippopotamus,
    the sorrows of the small!
He dropped two tears to mingle
    with the flowing Senegal;
And the 'Thank you' that he uttered
    was the saddest ever heard
In the Senegambian jungle
    from the mouth of beast or bird.

E. V. RIEU

[40]

Where Go the Boats?

Dark brown is the river,
   Golden is the sand.
It flows along for ever,
   With trees on either hand.

Green leaves a-floating,
   Castles of the foam,
Boats of mine a-boating –
   Where will all come home?

On goes the river
   And out past the mill,
Away down the valley,
   Away down the hill.

Away down the river,
   A hundred miles or more,
Other little children
   Shall bring my boats ashore.

ROBERT LOUIS STEVENSON

Dead Boy

The little cousin is dead, by foul subtraction,
A green bough from Virginia's aged tree,
And none of the county kin like the transaction,
Nor some of the world of outer dark, like me.

A boy not beautiful, nor good, nor clever,
A black cloud full of storms too hot for keeping,
A sword beneath his mother's heart – yet never
Woman bewept her babe as this is weeping.

A pig with a pasty face, so I had said,
Squealing for cookies, kinned by poor pretense
With a noble house. But the little man quite dead,
I see the forbears' antique lineaments.

The elder men have strode by the box of death
To the wide flag porch, and muttering low send round
The bruit of the day. O friendly waste of breath!
Their hearts are hurt with a deep dynastic wound.

He was pale and little, the foolish neighbors say;
The first-fruits, saith the Preacher, the Lord hath taken;
But this was the old tree's late branch wrenched away,
Grieving the sapless limbs, the shorn and shaken.

JOHN CROWE RANSOM

On Salathiel Pavy
(A child of Queen Elizabeth's Chapel)

Weep with me, all you that read
    This little story;
And know, for whom a tear you shed
    Death's self is sorry.
'Twas a child that so did thrive
    In grace and feature,
As Heaven and Nature seemed to strive
    Which owned the creature.

Years he numbered scarce thirteen
　　When Fates turned cruel,
Yet three filled Zodiacs had he been
　　The Stage's jewel;
And did act (what now we moan)
　　Old men so duly,
As sooth the Parcae[1] thought him one,
　　He played so truly.
So, by error, to his fate
　　They all consented;
But, viewing him since, alas, too late!
　　They have repented;
And have sought, to give new birth,
　　In baths to steep him;
But, being so much too good for earth,
　　Heaven vows to keep him.

BEN JONSON

[1]Fates

Boy at the Window

Seeing the snowman standing all alone
In dusk and cold is more than he can bear.
The small boy weeps to hear the wind prepare
A night of gnashings and enormous moan.
His tearful sight can hardly reach to where
The pale-faced figure with bitumen eyes
Returns him such a god-forsaken stare
As outcast Adam gave to Paradise.

The man of snow is, nonetheless, content,
Having no wish to go inside and die.
Still, he is moved to see the youngster cry.
Though frozen water is his element,
He melts enough to drop from one soft eye
A trickle of the purest rain, a tear
For the child at the bright pane surrounded by
Such warmth, such light, such love, and so much fear.

RICHARD WILBUR

Taxonomical Note

Not just the sizes named (like miniatures,
Littles, queens, King Kongs, dwarf alleys, alleys),
But patterns, lovingly, like silvers, clears,
Coca-colas, bottle-washers, genies,

Sparkle alleys, squids ('thick squirmy patterns',
Says my six-year-old), propellers, maypole
Alleys ('sort of stripy'), spiderwebs
And snowflake alleys ('they're most beautiful').

I tell you, there's a poet in this country.
He is probably eight years old. His head is full
Of coloured glass and words. He is a maker,
Unread, untutored, immemorial.

DAVID SUTTON

As you may guess, this is about a young collector of marbles.

Luriana, Lurilee

Come out and climb the garden path
   Luriana, Lurilee.
The China rose is all abloom
And buzzing with the yellow bee.
We'll swing you on the cedar bough,
   Luriana, Lurilee.

I wonder if it seems to you,
   Luriana, Lurilee,
That all the lives we ever lived
And all the lives to be,
Are full of trees and changing leaves,
   Luriana, Lurilee.

How long it seems since you and I,
   Luriana, Lurilee,
Roamed in the forest where our kind
Had just begun to be,
And laughed and chattered in the flowers,
   Luriana, Lurilee.

How long since you and I went out,
   Luriana, Lurilee,
To see the Kings go riding by
Over lawn and daisy lea,
With their palm leaves and cedar sheaves,
   Luriana, Lurilee.

Swing, swing, on the cedar bough,
  Luriana, Lurilee,
Till you sleep in a bramble heap
Or under a gloomy churchyard tree,
And then fly back to swing on a bough,
  Luriana, Lurilee.

CHARLES ELTON

Distracted the Mother Said to Her Boy

Distracted the mother said to her boy
'Do you try to upset and perplex and annoy?
Now, give me four reasons – and don't play the fool –
Why you shouldn't get up and get ready for school.'

Her son replied slowly, 'Well, mother, you see,
I can't stand the teachers and they detest me;
And there isn't a boy or a girl in the place
That I like or, in turn, that delights in my face.'

'And I'll give you two reasons,' she said, 'Why you ought
Get yourself off to school before you get caught;
Because, first, you are forty and, next, you young fool,
It's your job to be there.
You're the head of the school.'

GREGORY HARRISON

First Day at Boarding School

Like a trapped bird
she hid behind her hair.

Confident buxom girls
crowded the corridors

on their bedroom walls
pictures of pop-stars kissing.

What did they comprehend
of Africa's space and silence?

Like a caged animal
she sniffed the stuffy air,

heard the head's platitudes
resolved never to 'settle down',

pledged herself to wilderness
to bursting through closed doors

behind which they said
she must learn a new language.

PRUNELLA POWER

End of Term

Already the past's
a touched-up picture –
her London year.
She lies on the lawn
tape recorder beside her
concocting her version.

Grandmother, grand-daughter –
she's making a tape
to say she'll miss me.
I'm packing her bags,
leaving out lectures
hurts and displeasure.

Tomorrow she'll wake
above clouds in the sun
near parents and sister.
Tomorrow my house
will unravel and travel
back to its quietness.

PRUNELLA POWER

'A Midsummer Night's Dream' in Regent's Park

And what will they remember when
They wake, like Bottom, from their dream?
Will they believe they laughed like this?

And will their restless bodies seem
The same that settled here like dew
Along the benches, in a trance
Of hope and wonder, while old Puck
Led the four lovers through their dance?

The treetops rustle, and the sky
Darkens around a haughty moon.
Cartoon words on homespun lips
Float through the night in their balloon.
Titania curses Oberon
And up the loyal fairies leap.
Within a wood within a wood
The four enchanted lovers sleep.

And will these children ever think
Again about this leaf-lit scene –
Even a single turning branch
Glimmer in their darker green?
Perhaps one moment when the sky
Was dropping dusk light from above
Will touch their eyes with tenderness
Before another night of love.

DERWENT MAY

'So They Went Deeper into the Forest . . .'

'So they went deeper into the forest,' said Jacob Grimm,
And the child sat listening with all his ears,
While the angry queen passed. And in after years

The voice and the fall of words came back to him
(Though the fish and the faithful servant were grown dim,
The aproned witch, the door that disappears,
The lovely maid weeping delicious tears
And the youngest brother, with one bright-feathered limb) –
'Deeper into the forest.'
                                    There are oaks and beeches
And green high hollies. The multitudinous tree
Stands on the hill and clothes the valley, reaches
Over long lands, down to a roaring sea.
And the child moves onward, into the heart of the wood,
Unhindered, unresisted, unwithstood.

ROY DANIELLS

Song

I had a bicycle called 'Splendid',
A cricket-bat called 'The Rajah',
Eight box-kites and Scots soldiers
With kilts and red guns.
I had an album of postmarks,
A Longfellow with pictures,
Corduroy trousers that creaked,
A pencil with three colours.

Where do old things go to?
Could a cricket-bat be thrown away?
Where do the years go to?

ARTHUR WALEY

Twenty Years Ago

Round the house were lilacs and strawberries
   And foal-foots spangling the paths,
And far away on the sand-hills, dewberries
   Caught dust from the sea's long swaths.

Up in the wolds the woods were walking,
   And nuts fell out of their hair.
At the gate the nets hung, balking
   The star-lit rush of a hare.

In the autumn fields, the stubble
   Tinkled in music of gleaning.
At a mother's knee, the trouble
   Lost all its meaning.

Yea, what good beginnings
   To this sad end!
Have we had our innings?
   God forfend!

D. H. LAWRENCE

The Three Ravens

There were three ravens sat on a tree,
They were as black as they might be.

The one of them said to his make,[1]
'Where shall we our breakfast take?'

'Down in yonder greenè field
There lies a knight slain under his shield;

'His hounds they lie down at his feet,
So well do they their master keep;

'His hawks they flie so eagerly,
There's no fowl dare come him nigh.

'Down there comes a fallow doe
As great with young as she might goe.

'She lift up his bloudy head
And kist his wounds that were so red.

'She gat him up upon her back
And carried him to earthen lake.

[1]mate

'She buried him before the prime,
She was dead herself ere evensong time.

'God send every gentleman
Such hounds, such hawks, and such a leman!'

ANON

Edward, Edward

'Why does your brand sae drop wi' blude,
    Edward, Edward?
Why does your brand sae drop wi' blude,
    And why sae sad gang ye, O?' –
'O I hae kill'd my hawk sae gude,
    Mither, mither;
O I hae kill'd my hawk sae gude,
    And I had nae mair but he, O.'

'Your hawk's blude was never sae red,
    Edward, Edward;
Your hawk's blude was never sae red,
    My dear son, I tell thee, O.' –
'O I hae kill'd my red-roan steed,
    Mither, mither;
O I hae kill'd my red-roan steed,
    That erst was sae fair and free, O.'

'Your steed was auld, and ye hae got mair,
  Edward, Edward;
Your steed was auld, and ye hae got mair;
  Some other dule ye dree, O.'[1]
'O I hae kill'd my father dear,
  Mither, mither;
O I hae kill'd my father dear,
  Alas, and wae is me, O!'

'And whatten penance will ye dree[2] for that,
  Edward, Edward?
Whatten penance will ye dree for that?
  My dear son, now tell me, O.' –
'I'll set my feet in yonder boat,
  Mither, mither;
'I'll set my feet in yonder boat,
  And I'll fare over the sea, O.'

'And what will ye do wi' your tow'rs and your ha',
  Edward, Edward?
And what will ye do wi' your tow'rs and your ha',
  That were sae fair to see, O?' –
'I'll let them stand till they doun fa',
  Mither, mither;
I'll let them stand till they doun fa',
  For here never mair maun I be, O.'

'And what will ye leave to your bairns and your wife,
  Edward, Edward?
And what will ye leave to your bairns and your wife,
  When ye gang owre the sea, O?' –
'The warld's room: let them beg through life;
  Mither, mither;
The warld's room: let them beg through life;
  For them never mair will I see, O.'

[1]grief you suffer   [2]endure

'And what will ye leave to your ain mither dear,
   Edward, Edward?
And what will ye leave to your ain mither dear,
   My dear son, now tell me, O?' –
'The curse of hell frae me sall ye bear,
   Mither, mither;
The curse of hell frae me sall ye bear:
   Sic counsels ye gave to me, O!'

ANON

There Was a Knight

There was a knicht riding frae the east,
   Jennifer gentle an' rosemaree.
Who had been wooing at monie a place,
   As the doo[1] flies owre the mulberry tree.

He cam' unto a widow's door,
And speird[2] whare her three dochters were.

'The auldest ane's to a washing gane,
The second's to a baking gane.

'The youngest ane's to a wedding gane,
And it will be nicht or[3] she be hame.'

He sat him doun upon a stane,
Till thir three lasses cam' tripping hame.

The auldest ane she let him in,
And pinned the door wi' a siller pin.

[1]dove   [2]asked   [3]ere

The second ane she made his bed,
And laid saft pillows unto his head.

The youngest ane was bauld[1] and bricht,
And she tarried for words wi' this unco[2] knicht. –

'Gin ye will answer me questions ten,
The morn ye sall be made my ain: –

'O what is higher nor[3] the tree?
And what is deeper nor the sea?

'Or what is heavier nor the lead?
And what is better nor the bread?

'Or what is whiter nor the milk?
Or what is safter nor the silk?

'Or what is sharper nor a thorn?
Or what is louder nor a horn?

'Or what is greener nor the grass?
Or what is waur[4] nor a woman was?'

'O heaven is higher nor the tree,
And hell is deeper nor the sea.

'O sin is heavier nor the lead,
The blessing's better nor the bread.

'The snaw is whiter nor the milk,
And the down is safter nor the silk.

'Hunger is sharper nor a thorn,
And shame is louder nor a horn.

'The pies[5] are greener nor the grass,
And Clootie's waur nor a woman was.'

[1]bold [2]strange [3]than [4]worse [5]woodpeckers

As sune as she the fiend did name,
   Jennifer gentle an' rosemaree,
He flew awa' in a blazing flame,
   As the doo flies owre the mulberry tree.

ANON

Proud Maisie

Proud Maisie is in the wood,
   Walking so early;
Sweet Robin sits on the bush,
   Singing so rarely.

'Tell me, thou bonny bird,
   When shall I marry me?'
'When six braw gentlemen
   Kirkward shall carry ye.'

'Who makes the bridal bed,
   Birdie, say truly?'
'The grey-headed sexton
   That delves the grave duly.'

'The glow-worm o'er grave and stone
   Shall light thee steady;
The owl from the steeple sing
   Welcome, proud lady.'

SIR WALTER SCOTT

The Lament of the Border Widow

My love he built me a bonny bower,
And clad it a' wi' lilye flour;
A brawer bower ye ne'er did see,
Than my true love he built for me.

There came a man, by middle day,
He spied his sport, and went away;
And brought the King that very night,
Who brake my bower, and slew my knight.

He slew my knight, to me sae dear;
He slew my knight, and poin'd[1] his gear;
My servants all for life did flee,
And left me in extremitie.

I sew'd his sheet, making my mane[2];
I watch'd the corpse, myself alane;
I watch'd his body, night and day;
No living creature came that way.

I took his body on my back,
And whiles[3] I gaed, and whiles I sat;
I digg'd a grave, and laid him in,
And happ'd him with the sod sae green.

But think na ye my heart was sair,
When I laid the moul' on his yellow hair;
O think na ye my heart was wae,
When I turn'd about, away to gae;

[1]made forfeit [2]moan [3]sometimes

[59]

Nae living man I'll love again,
Since that my lovely knight is slain;
Wi' ae lock of his yellow hair
I'll chain my heart for evermair.

ANON

From The High Tide on the Coast of Lincolnshire, 1571

The old mayor climb'd the belfry tower,
  The ringers ran by two, by three;
'Pull, if ye never pull'd before;
  Good ringers, pull your best,' quoth he.
'Play uppe, play uppe, O Boston bells!
Ply all your changes, all your swells,
  Play uppe "The Brides of Enderby".'

Men say it was a stolen tyde –
  The Lord that sent it, He knows all;
But in myne ears doth still abide
  The message that the bells let fall:
And there was naught of strange, beside
The flights of mews and peewits pied
  By millions crouch'd on the old sea wall.

I sat and spun within the doore,
  My thread brake off, I raised myne eyes;
The level sun, like ruddy ore,
  Lay sinking in the barren skies,
And dark against day's golden death
She moved where Lindis wandereth,
My sonne's fair wife, Elizabeth.

'Cusha! Cusha! Cusha!' calling,
Ere the early dews were falling,
Farre away I heard her song.
'Cusha! Cusha!' all along
Where the reedy Lindis floweth,
  Floweth, floweth;
From the meads where melick groweth
Faintly came her milking song . . .

If it be long, ay, long ago,
  When I beginne to think howe long,
Againe I hear the Lindis flow,
  Swift as an arrowe, sharp and strong;
And all the aire, it seemeth mee,
Bin full of floating bells (sayth shee),
That ring the tune of Enderby.

Alle fresh the level pasture lay,
  And not a shadowe mote be seene,
Save where full fyve good miles away
  The steeple tower'd from out the greene;
And lo! the great bell farre and wide
Was heard in all the country side
That Saturday at eventide. . . .

Then some look'd uppe into the sky,
  And all along where Lindis flows
To where the goodly vessels lie,
  And where the lordly steeple shows.
They sayde, 'And why should this thing be?
What danger lowers by land or sea?
They ring the tune of Enderby!'

I look'd without, and lo! my sonne
  Came riding downe with might and main:
He raised a shout as he drew on,
  Till all the welkin rang again. . . .

'The olde sea wall (he cried) is downe,
  The rising tide comes on apace,
And boats adrift in yonder towne
  Go sailing uppe the market-place.'
He shook as one that looks on death:
  'God save you, mother!' straight he saith;
'Where is my wife, Elizabeth?'

'Good sonne, where Lindis winds away,
  With her two bairns I mark'd her long;
And ere yon bells beganne to play
  Afar I heard her milking song.'
He looked across the grassy lea,
To right, to left, 'Ho Enderby!'
They rang 'The Brides of Enderby!'

With that he cried and beat his breast;
  For, lo! along the river's bed
A mighty eygre reared his crest,
  And uppe the Lindis raging sped.
It swept with thunderous noises loud;
Shaped like a curling snow-white cloud,
Or like a demon in a shroud.

And rearing Lindis backward press'd
  Shook all her trembling bankes amaine;
Then madly at the eygre's breast
  Flung uppe her weltering walls again.
Then bankes came downe with ruin and rout –
Then beaten foam flew round about –
Then all the mighty floods were out.

So farre, so fast the eygre drave,
  The heart had hardly time to beat,
Before a shallow seething wave
  Sobbed in the grasses at oure feet:
The feet had hardly time to flee
Before it brake against the knee,
And all the world was in the sea.

Upon the roofe we sate that night,
  The noise of bells went sweeping by;
I mark'd the lofty beacon light
  Stream from the church tower, red and high –
A lurid mark and dread to see;
And awsome bells they were to mee,
That in the dark rang 'Enderby'.

They rang the sailor lads to guide
  From roofe to roofe who fearless row'd;
And I – my sonne was at my side,
  And yet the ruddy beacon glow'd;
And yet he moan'd beneath his breath,
'O come in life, or come in death!
O lost! my love, Elizabeth.'

And didst thou visit him no more?
   Thou didst, thou didst, my daughter deare;
The waters laid thee at his doore,
   Ere yet the early dawn was clear.
Thy pretty bairns in fast embrace,
The lifted sun shone on thy face,
Downe drifted to thy dwelling-place.

That flow strew'd wrecks about the grass,
That ebbe swept out the flocks to sea;
A fatal ebbe and flow, alas!
   To manye more than myne and mee:
But each will mourn his own (she saith),
And sweeter woman ne'er drew breath
Than my sonne's wife, Elizabeth. . . .

I shall never see her more
Where the reeds and rushes quiver,
   Shiver, quiver;
Stand beside the sobbing river,
Sobbing, throbbing, in its falling
To the sandy lonesome shore;
I shall never hear her calling,
Leave your meadow grasses mellow,
   Mellow, mellow;
Quit your cowslips, cowslips yellow;
Come uppe Whitefoot, come uppe Lightfoot;
Quit your pipes of parsley hollow,
   Hollow, hollow;
Come uppe Lightfoot, rise and follow;
   Lightfoot, Whitefoot,
From your clovers lift the head;
Come uppe Jetty, follow, follow,
Jetty, to the milking shed.

JEAN INGELOW

[64]

Hiawatha's Canoe

'Give me of your bark, O Birch-tree!
Of your yellow bark, O Birch-tree!
Growing by the rushing river,
Tall and stately in the valley!
I a light canoe will build me,
Build a swift Cheemaun[1] for sailing,
That shall float upon the river,
Like a yellow leaf in Autumn,
Like a yellow water-lily.
  'Lay aside your cloak, O Birch-tree!
Lay aside your white-skin wrapper,
For the Summer-time is coming,
And the sun is warm in heaven,
And you need no white-skin wrapper!'
  Thus aloud cried Hiawatha.

And the tree with all its branches
Rustled in the breeze of morning,
Saying, with a sigh of patience,
  'Take my cloak, O Hiawatha!'
  With his knife the tree he girdled;
Just beneath its lowest branches,
Just above the roots he cut it,
Till the sap came oozing outward;
Down the trunk from top to bottom,
Sheer he cleft the back asunder,
With a wooden wedge he raised it,
Stripped it from the trunk unbroken.

[1]birch canoe

'Give me of your boughs, O Cedar!
Of your strong and pliant branches,
My canoe to make more steady,
Make more strong and firm beneath me!'
   Through the summit of the Cedar
Went a sound, a cry of horror,
Went a murmur of resistance;
But it whispered, bending downward,
   'Take my boughs, O Hiawatha!'
   Down he hewed the boughs of cedar,
Shaped them straightway to a frame-work,
Like two bows he formed and shaped them,
Like two bended bows together.

   'Give me of your roots, O Tamarack!
Of your fibrous roots, O Larch-tree!
My canoe to bind together,
So to bind the ends together
That the water may not enter,
That the river may not wet me!'
   And the Larch, with all its fibres,
Shivered in the air of morning,
Touched his forehead with its tassels,
Said, with one long sigh of sorrow,
   'Take them all, O Hiawatha!'
   From the earth he tore the fibres,
Tore the tough roots of the Larch-tree,
Closely sewed the bark together,
Bound it closely to the frame-work.

   'Give me of your balm, O Fir-tree!
Of your balsam and your resin,
So to close the seams together
That the water may not enter,
That the river may not wet me!'

And the Fir-tree tall and sombre,
Sobbed through all its robes of darkness,
Rattled like a shore with pebbles,
Answered wailing, answered weeping,
   'Take my balm, O Hiawatha!'
   And he took the tears of balsam,
Took the resin of the Fir-tree,
Smeared therewith each seam and fissure
Made each crevice safe from water.

   'Give me of your quills, O Hedgehog!
All your quills, O Kagh, the Hedgehog!
I will make a necklace of them,
Make a girdle for my beauty,
And two stars to deck her bosom!'
   From a hollow tree the Hedgehog
With his sleepy eyes looked at him,
Shot his shining quills, like arrows,
Saying with a drowsy murmur,
Through the tangle of his whiskers,
   'Take my quills, O Hiawatha!'
   From the ground the quills he gathered,
All the little shining arrows,
Stained them red and blue and yellow,
With the juice of roots and berries;
Into his canoe he wrought them,
Round its waist a shining girdle,
Round its bows a gleaming necklace,
On its breast two stars resplendent.

Thus the Birch Canoe was builded,
In the valley, by the river,
In the bosom of the forest;
And the forest's life was in it,
All its mystery and its magic,
All the lightness of the birch-tree,

All the toughness of the cedar,
All the larch's supple sinews;
And it floated on the river
Like a yellow leaf in Autumn,
Like a yellow water-lily.

H. W. LONGFELLOW
from *The Song of Hiawatha*

The Twins

'Give' and 'It-shall-be-given-unto-you.'

Grand rough old Martin Luther
   Bloomed fables – flowers on furze,
The better the uncouther:
   Do roses stick like burrs?

A beggar asked an alms
   One day at an abbey-door,
Said Luther; but, seized with qualms,
   The Abbot replied, 'We're poor!

'Poor, who had plenty once,
   When gifts fell thick as rain;
But they give us nought, for the nonce,
   And how should we give again?'

Then the beggar, 'See your sins!
   Of old, unless I err,
Ye had brothers for inmates, twins,
   Date and Dabitur.[1]

[1]See the sub-title.

'While Date was in good case
    Dabitur flourished too:
For Dabitur's lenten face,
    No wonder if Date rue.

'Would ye retrieve the one?
    Try and make plump the other!
When Date's penance is done,
    Dabitur helps his brother.

'Only, beware relapse!'
    The Abbot hung his head.
This beggar might be, perhaps,
    An angel, Luther said.

ROBERT BROWNING

St Martin and the Beggar

Martin sat young upon his bed
A budding cenobite,
Said 'Though I hold the principles
Of Christian life be right,
I cannot grow from them alone,
I must go out to fight.'

He travelled hard, he travelled far,
The light began to fail.
'Is not this act of mine,' he said,
'A cowardly betrayal,
Should I not peg my nature down
With a religious nail?'

Wind scudded on the marshland,
And, dangling at his side,
His sword soon clattered under hail:
What could he do but ride? –
There was not shelter for a dog,
The garrison far ahead.

A ship that moves on darkness
He rode across the plain,
When a brawny beggar started up
Who pulled at his rein
And leant dripping with sweat and water
Upon the horse's mane.

He glared into Martin's eyes
With eyes more wild than bold;
His hair sent rivers down his spine;
Like a fowl plucked to be sold
His flesh was grey. Martin said –
'What, naked in this cold?

'I have no food to give you,
Money would be a joke.'
Pulling his new sword from the sheath
He took his soldier's cloak
And cut it in two equal parts
With a single stroke.

Grabbing one to his shoulders,
Pinning it with his chin,
The beggar dived into the dark,
And soaking to the skin
Martin went on slowly
Until he reached an inn.

One candle on the wooden table,
The food and drink were poor,
The woman hobbled off, he ate,
Then casually before
The table stood the beggar as
If he had used the door.

Now dry, for hair and flesh had been
By warm airs fanned,
Still bare but round each muscled thigh
A single golden band,
His eyes now wild with love, he held
The half cloak in his hand.

'You recognised the human need
Included yours, because
You did not hesitate, my saint,
To cut your cloak across;
But never since that moment
Did you regret the loss.

'My enemies would have turned away,
My holy toadies would
Have given all the cloak and frozen
Conscious that they were good.
But you, being a saint of men,
Gave only what you could.'

St Martin stretched his hand out
To offer from his plate,
But the beggar vanished, thinking food
Like cloaks is needless weight.
Pondering on the matter,
St Martin bent and ate.

THOM GUNN

Christmas at Sea

The sheets were frozen hard, and they cut the naked hand;
The decks were like a slide, where a seaman scarce could
    stand;
The wind was a nor'wester, blowing squally off the sea;
And cliffs and spouting breakers were the only things a-lee.

They heard the surf a-roaring before the break of day;
But 'twas only with the peep of light we saw how ill we lay.
We tumbled every hand on deck instanter, with a shout,
And we gave her the maintops'l, and stood by to go about.

All day we tacked and tacked between the South Head and
    the North;
All day we hauled the frozen sheets, and got no further
    forth;
All day as cold as charity, in bitter pain and dread,
For very life and nature we tacked from head to head.

We gave the South a wider berth, for there the tide-race
    roared;
But every tack we made we brought the North Head close
    aboard:
So's we saw the cliffs and houses, and the breakers running
    high,
And the coastguard in his garden, with his glass against his
    eye.

The frost was on the village roofs as white as ocean foam;
The good red fires were burning bright in every 'longshore
    home;
The windows sparkled clear, and the chimneys volleyed
    out;
And I vow we sniffed the victuals as the vessel went about.

The bells upon the church were rung with a mighty jovial
    cheer
For it's just that I should tell you how (of all days in the year)
This day of our adversity was blessèd Christmas morn,
And the house above the coastguard's was the house where
    I was born.

O well I saw the pleasant room, the pleasant faces there,
My mother's silver spectacles, my father's silver hair;
And well I saw the firelight, like a flight of homely elves,
Go dancing round the china-plates that stand upon the
    shelves.

And well I knew the talk they had, the talk that was of me,
Of the shadow on the household and the son that went to
    sea;
And O the wicked fool! I seemed, in every kind of way,
To be here and hauling frozen ropes on blessèd Christmas
    Day.

They lit the high sea-light, and the dark began to fall.
'All hands to loose topgallant sails,' I heard the captain call,
'By the Lord, she'll never stand it,' our first mate, Jackson,
    cried.
. . . 'It's the one way or the other, Mr. Jackson,' he replied.

She staggered to her bearings, but the sails were new and
    good.
And the ship smelt up to windward just as though she
    understood.
As the winter's day was ending, in the entry of the night,
We cleared the weary headland, and passed below the light.

And they heaved a mighty breath, every soul on board but
   me,
As they saw her nose again pointing handsome out to sea;
But all that I could think of, in the darkness and the cold,
Was just that I was leaving home and my folks were
   growing old.

ROBERT LOUIS STEVENSON

At a Pause in a Country Dance
(Middle of Last Century)

They stood at the foot of the figure,
And panted: they'd danced it down through –
That 'Dashing White Serjeant' they loved so: –
A window, uncurtained was nigh them
That end of the room. Thence in view

Outside it a valley updrew,
Where the frozen moon lit frozen snow:
At the furthermost reach of the valley
A light from a window shone low.
'They are inside that window,' said she,

As she looked. 'They sit up there for me;
And baby is sleeping there, too.'
He glanced. 'Yes,' he said. 'Never mind,
Let's foot our way up again; do!
And dance down the line as before.

[74]

'What's the world to us, meeting once more!'
'– Not much, when your husband full trusts you,
And thinks the child his that I bore!'
He was silent. The fiddlers six-eighted
With even more passionate vigour.

The pair swept again up the figure,
The child's cuckoo-father and she,
And the next couples threaded below,
And the twain wove their way to the top
Of 'The Dashing White Serjeant' they loved so,
Restarting: right, left, to and fro.

– From the homestead, seen yon, the small glow
Still adventured forth over the white,
Where the child slept, unknowing who sired it,
In the cradle of wicker tucked tight,
And its grandparents, nodding, admired it
In elbow-chairs through the slow night.

THOMAS HARDY

Silent is the House

Silent is the house: all are laid asleep:
One alone looks out o'er the snow-wreaths deep,
Watching every cloud, dreading every breeze
That whirls the wildering drift and bends the groaning trees.

Cheerful is the hearth, soft the matted floor;
Not one shivering gust creeps through pen or door;
The little lamp burns straight, its rays shoot strong and far:
I trim it well, to be the wanderer's guiding-star.

Frown, my haughty sire; chide, my angry dame;
Set your slaves to spy; threaten me with shame!
But neither sire, nor dame, nor prying serf shall know,
What angel nightly tracks that waste of frozen snow.

What I love shall come like visitant of air,
Safe in secret power from lurking human snare;
What loves me, no word of mine shall e'er betray,
Though for faith unstained my life must forfeit pay.

Burn, then, little lamp; glimmer straight and clear –
Hush! a rustling wing stirs, methinks, the air:
He for whom I wait, thus ever comes to me;
Strange Power! I trust thy might; trust thou my constancy.

EMILY BRONTË

These well-known lines are in fact the prelude to a very long,
mysterious ballad, one of the most haunting and extraordinary
poems that Emily Brontë ever wrote.

Angels, Demons, Phantoms, Dreams

Lucifer in Starlight

On a starred night Prince Lucifer uprose.
Tired of his dark dominion swung the fiend
Above the rolling ball in cloud part screened,
Where sinners hugged their spectre of repose.
Poor prey to his hot fit of pride were those.
And now upon his western wing he leaned,
Now his huge bulk o'er Afric's sands careened,
Now the black planet shadowed Arctic snows.
Soaring through wider zones that pricked his scars
With memory of the old revolt from Awe,
He reached a middle height, and at the stars,
Which are the brain of heaven, he looked, and sank.
Around the ancient track marched rank on rank
The army of unalterable law.

GEORGE MEREDITH

Birkett's Eagle

Adam Birkett took his gun
  And climbed from Wasdale Head;
He swore he could spare no more lambs
  To keep an eagle fed.

[77]

So Birkett went along the Trod
    That climbs by Gavel Neese,
Till on his right stood Gavel Crag,
    And leftward fell the screes.

The mist whirled up from Ennerdale,
    And Gavel Crag grew dim,
And from the rocks on Birkett's right
    The eagle spoke to him.

'What ails you, Adam Birkett,
    That you have climbed so far
To make an end of Lucifer,
    That was the Morning Star?

'If there's a heaven, Birkett,
    There's certainly a hell;
And he who would kill Lucifer
    Destroys himself as well.'

The mist whirled off from Gavel Crag,
    And swept towards Beck Head,
And Adam Birkett took his aim
    And shot the eagle dead.

He looked down into Ennerdale
    To where its body fell,
And at his back stood Gavel Crag,
    And at his feet lay Hell.

Birkett scrambled off the rocks,
    And back onto the Trod,
And on his right lay Ennerdale,
    And on his left stood God.

'What was it, Adam Birkett,
    That fell onto the scree?
For I feared it might be Lucifer
    That once was dear to me.

'And from Carlisle to Ravenglass,
    From Shap to St Bees Head,
There's nobody worth vanquishing
    If Lucifer is dead.'

Birkett's dogs leapt all about
    As he came down the scree,
But he said 'I have killed Lucifer,
    And what is left for me?'

Birkett's lambs leapt all about
    As he came off the fell,
But he said 'I have killed Lucifer,
    And I am dead as well.'

But Lucifer the Morning Star
    Walked thoughtfully away
From the screes beyond the Gavel
    Where the eagle's body lay.

And as he went by Black Sail Pass
    And round below Kirk Fell,
He looked like young Tom Ritson
    Who knew the Birketts well.

And he came down to Wasdale Head,
    Young Ritson to the life,
With an apple in his pocket
    Which he gave to Birkett's wife.

DOROTHY S. HOWARD

Tom's Angel

No one was in the fields
But me and Polly Flint,
When, like a giant across the grass,
The flaming angel went.

It was budding time in May,
And green as green could be,
And all in his height he went along
Past Polly Flint and me.

We'd been playing in the woods,
And Polly up, and ran,
And hid her face, and said,
'Tom! Tom! The Man! The Man!'

And I up-turned; and there,
Like flames across the sky,
With wings all bristling, came
The Angel striding by.

And a chaffinch overhead
Kept whistling in the tree
While the Angel, blue as fire, came on
Past Polly Flint and me.

And I saw his hair, and all
The ruffling of his hem,
As over the clovers his bare feet
Trod without stirring them.

Polly – she cried; and, oh!
We ran, until the lane
Turned by the miller's roaring wheel,
And we were safe again.

WALTER DE LA MARE

[80]

A Little East of Jordan

A little East of Jordan,
Evangelists record,
A Gymnast and an Angel
Did wrestle long and hard –

Till morning touching mountain –
And Jacob, waxing strong,
The Angel begged permission
To Breakfast – to return –

Not so, said cunning Jacob!
'I will not let thee go
Except thou bless me' – Stranger!
The which acceded to –

Light swung the silver fleeces
'Peniel' Hills beyond,
And the bewildered Gymnast
Found he had worsted God!

EMILY DICKINSON

From the Coptic

Three angels came to the red red clay
Where in a heap it formless lay,

Stand up, stand up, thou lazy red clay,
Stand up and be Man this happy day.

Oh in its bones the red clay groaned,
And why should I do such a thing? it said,
And take such a thing on my downy head?
Then the first angel stood forth and said,

Thou shalt have happiness, thou shalt have pain,
And each shall fall turn and about again,
And no man shall say when the day shall fall
That thou shalt be happy or not at all.

And the second angel said much the same
While the red clay lay flat in the falling rain,
Crying, I will stay clay and take no blame.

Then the third angel rose up and said,
Listen thou clay, raise thy downy head,
When thou hast heard what I have to say
Thou shalt rise Man and go man's way.

What have you to promise? the red clay moans,
What have you in store for my future bones?
I am Death, said the angel, and death is the end,
I am Man, cries clay rising, and you are my friend.

STEVIE SMITH

Angels

have you noticed
how they roost in trees?
not like birds
their wings fold the other way

my mother, whose eyes are clouding
gets up early to shoo them
out of her pippin tree
afraid they will let go their droppings
over the lovely olive
of the runnelled bark

she keeps a broom by the door
brushes them from the branches
not too gently
go and lay eggs she admonishes

they clamber down
jump clumsily to the wet ground
while she makes clucking noises
to encourage them to the nest

does not notice how they
bow down low before her anger
each lifting a cold and rosy hand
from beneath the white feathers
raising it in greeting
blessing her and the air
as they back away into the mist

ANNE SZUMIGALSKI

Conversation with an Angel

On my way to Sainsbury's
I met an Angel. He stood
relaxed, one foot and one wing
off the pavement, waiting
for me to pass. I stopped
to see if he needed anything: had he
lost his way? Could I help perhaps?
No, he lacked nothing, simply wanted
some contact with the world again;
he'd been human once and he sometimes
craved that bitter-sweet flavour . . .
Some angels were born – he explained –
others translated. Could I
become an angel? Was there a waiting list?
Not a chance for you, he laughed,
no one who has seen
an angel can ever become one.

WANDA BARFORD

Café

A pair of angels
Were quietly settling down.
    How did they look?
They had six wings like seraphim,
And brilliant eyes, like butterflies.
I left them to finish my coffee:
    Too sweet for me,
    And not too black for them.

HALA BAYKOV

From The Children of Stare

Winter is fallen early
On the house of Stare;
Birds in reverberating flocks
Haunt its ancestral box;
Bright are the plenteous berries
In clusters in the air. . . .

'Tis strange to see young children
In such a wintry house;
Like rabbits' on the frozen snow
Their tell-tale footprints go;
Their laughter rings like timbrels
'Neath evening ominous. . . .

Above them silence lours,
Still as an arctic sea;
Light fails; night falls; the wintry moon
Glitters; the crocus soon
Will open grey and distracted
On earth's austerity:

Thick mystery, wild peril,
Law like an iron rod: –
Yet sport they on in Spring's attire,
Each with his tiny fire
Blown to a core of ardour
By the awful breath of God.

WALTER DE LA MARE

The Brothers

Last night I watched my brothers play,
The gentle and the reckless one,
In a field two yards away.
For half a century they were gone
Beyond the other side of care
To be among the peaceful dead.
Even in a dream how could I dare
Interrogate that happiness
So wildly spent yet never less?
For still they raced about the green
And were like two revolving suns;
A brightness poured from head to head,
So strong I could not see their eyes
Or look into their paradise.
What were they doing, the happy ones?
Yet where I was they once had been.

I thought, How could I be so dull,
Twenty thousand days ago,
Not to see they were beautiful?
I asked them, Were you really so
As you are now, that other day?
And the dream was soon away.

For then we played for victory
And not to make each other glad.
A darkness covered every head,
Frowns twisted the original face,
And through that mask we could not see
The beauty and the buried grace.

I have observed in foolish awe
The dateless mid-days of the law
And seen indifferent justice done
By everyone on everyone.
And in a vision I have seen
My brothers playing on the green.

EDWIN MUIR

Midnight

Midnight
The graveyard is silent.
The howling wind rushes by.
I hear a noise and spin around,
around and around.
There it is again; tap, tap, tap,
Looking behind a gravestone,
I see a vision of a man.
With a hammer and chisel
I ask him what he is doing,
He replies, 'They spelt my name wrong.'

BALJIT KANG (11)

Hallowe'en

On Hallowe'en the old ghosts come
About us, and they speak to some;
To others they are dumb.

They haunt the hearts that loved them best;
In some they are by grief possessed,
In other hearts they rest.

They have a knowledge they would tell;
To some of us it is a knell,
To some, a miracle.

They come unseen and go unseen;
And some will never know they've been,
And some will know all they mean.

ELEANOR FARJEON

The Garden Seat

Its former green is blue and thin,
And its once firm legs sink in and in;
Soon it will break down unaware,
Soon it will break down unaware.

At night when reddest flowers are black
Those who once sat thereon come back;
Quite a row of them sitting there,
Quite a row of them sitting there.

With them the seat does not break down,
Nor winter freeze them, nor floods drown,
For they are as light as upper air,
They are as light as upper air!

THOMAS HARDY

When the Eye of Day is Shut

When the eye of day is shut,
   And the stars deny their beams,
And about the forest hut
   Blows the roaring wood of dreams,

From deep clay, from desert rock,
   From the sunk sands of the main,
Come not at my door to knock,
   Hearts that loved me not again.

Sleep, be still, turn to your rest
   In the lands where you are laid;
In far lodgings east and west
   Lie down on the beds you made.

In gross marl, in blowing dust,
   In the drowned ooze of the sea,
Where you would not, lie you must,
   Lie you must, and not with me.

A. E. HOUSMAN

Chatterton

Out of the swirling shadow host
I called to hear my rhyme
He came. A man? A dream? A ghost?
Me, in past time?

At first he stood beside my chair
And listened with the rest
And then he whispered in my ear –
His words were best.

He did not go. He shared my bed
Part of my blood and bone,
He felt my feelings, ruled my head,
Till we were one.

We sang: our voice was true and strong.
We wrote: he held the pen
Until he wished, to hear our song,
Not dreams, but men.

Men took him from me, and he took
The only life I know.
Shorn of the life that I foresook,
To death I go.

RINA HANDS

Thomas Chatterton (1752–1770), a Bristol boy, spent his short life during the only 'Classical' period of English writing, when no Romantic work was acceptable unless disguised as a 'found' ancient manuscript. In order to write his quite remarkable poems (most are in his verse drama *Aella*, written when he was fifteen and sixteen) he assumed the identity of a fifteenth-century Bristol scribe and cleric, Thomas Rowley. (This explains his curious words and spellings: see poems on pages 96 and 135.) Feeling a failure, he took his life in a Holborn garret three months before he was eighteen, and became a romantic symbol, 'the marvellous boy', for generations of poets thereafter. A Pre-Raphaelite painting, 'The Death of Chatterton', young George Meredith serving as a model, is in the Tate Gallery.

Columbus

To find the Western path,
Right thro' the Gates of Wrath . . .
                              BLAKE

As I walked with my friend,
My singular Columbus,
Where the land comes to an end
And the path is perilous,
Where the wheel and tattered shoe
And bottle have been thrown,
And the sky is shining blue,
And the heart sinks like a stone,

I plucked his sleeve and said,
'I have come far to find
The springs of a broken bed,
The ocean, and the wind.
I'd rather live in Greece,
Castile, or an English town
Than wander here like this
Where the dunes come tumbling down.'

He answered me, 'Perhaps.
But Europe never guessed
America, their maps
Could not describe the West.
And though in Plato's glass
The stars were still and clear,
Yet nothing came to pass
And men died of despair.'

He said, 'If there is not
A way to China, one
City surpassing thought,
My ghost will still go on.
I'll spread the airy sail.'
He said, 'and point the sprit
To a country that cannot fail,
For there's no finding it.'

Straightway we separated –
He, in his fading coat,
To the water's edge, where waited
An admiral's longboat.
A crew of able seamen
Sprang up at his command –
An angel or a demon –
And they rowed him from the land.

LOUIS SIMPSON

The Dream about Our Master, William Shakespeare

This midnight dream whispered to me:
*Be swift as a runner, take the lane
Into the green mystery
Beyond the farm and haystack at Stone.
You leave tomorrow, not to return.*

Hands that were fastened in a vise,
A useless body, rooted foot,
While time like a bell thundered the loss,
Witnessed the closing of the gate.
Thus sleep and waking both betrayed.

I had one glimpse: In a close of shadow
There rose the form of a manor-house.
And in a corner a curtained window.
All was lost in a well of trees,
Yet I knew for certain this was the place.

If the hound of air, the ropes of shade,
And the gate between that is no gate,
Had not so held me and delayed
These cowardly limbs of bone and blood,
I would have met him as he lived!

HYAM PLUTZIK

To Make a Prairie

To make a prairie it takes a clover and one bee,
One clover, and a bee,
And revery.
The revery alone will do,
If bees are few.

EMILY DICKINSON

All Hushed and Still within the House

All hushed and still within the house;
Without – all wind and driving rain;
But something whispers to my mind,
Through rain and through the wailing wind,
    Never again.
Never again? Why not again?
Memory has power as real as thine.

EMILY BRONTË

Dreams

My dreams are lucid.
They must be someone else's;
I'm not so clever.

ANNE BLOCH

(*Haiku*)

The Wild, the Tamed

Spring

Spring, the sweet spring, is the year's pleasant king;
Then blooms each thing, then maids dance in a ring,
Cold doth not sting, the pretty birds do sing:
Cuckoo, jug-jug, pu-we, to-witta-woo!

The palm and may make country houses gay,
Lambs frisk and play, the shepherds pipe all day,
And we hear aye birds tune this merry lay:
   Cuckoo, jug-jug, pu-we, to-witta-woo!

The fields breathe sweet, the daisies kiss our feet,
Young lovers meet, old wives a-sunning sit;
In every street these tunes our ears do greet:
   Cuckoo, jug-jug, pu-we, to-witta-woo!
     Spring, the sweet spring!

THOMAS NASHE

Summer Dawn

Pray but one prayer for me 'twixt thy closed lips,
Think but one thought of me up in the stars.
The summer night waneth, the morning light slips
    Faint and gray 'twixt the leaves of the aspen, betwixt the
      cloud-bars,
That are patiently waiting there for the dawn:
    Patient and colourless, though Heaven's gold
Waits to float through them along with the sun.
Far out in the meadows, above the young corn,
    The heavy elms wait, and restless and cold
The uneasy wind rises; the roses are dun;
Through the long twilight they pray for the dawn
Round the lone house in the midst of the corn.
      Speak but one word to me over the corn,
      Over the tender, bow'd locks of the corn.

WILLIAM MORRIS

Autumn

When Autumn bleak and sunburnt do appear,
    With his gold hand gilding the falling leaf,
Bringing up Winter to fulfil the year,
    Bearing upon his back the ripèd sheaf,
When all the hills with woody seed is white,
When levin[1]-fires and lemes[2] do meet from far the sight;

[1]lightning   [2]gleams

When the fair apple, red as even sky,
   Do bend the tree unto the fruitful ground.
When juicy pears, and berries of black dye,
   Do dance in air, and call the eyes around;
Then, be the even foul, or even fair,
Methinks my hartys joy is steyncèd[1] with some care.

THOMAS CHATTERTON
from *Aella*

[1] mingled   See note on page 90

To Autumn

Season of mists and mellow fruitfulness,
   Close bosom-friend of the maturing sun;
Conspiring with him how to load and bless
   With fruit the vines that round the thatch-eaves run;
To bend with apples the mossed cottage-trees,
   And fill all fruit with ripeness to the core;
      To swell the gourd, and plump the hazel shells
With a sweet kernel; to set budding more,
And still more, later flowers for the bees,
Until they think warm days will never cease,
      For Summer has o'er-brimmed their clammy cells –

Who hath not seen thee oft amid thy store?
   Sometimes whoever seeks abroad may find
Thee sitting careless on a granary floor,
   Thy hair soft-lifted by the winnowing wind;
Or on a half-reaped furrow sound asleep,
   Drowsed with the fume of poppies, while thy hook
      Spares the next swath and all its twinèd flowers:

And sometimes like a gleaner thou dost keep
   Steady thy laden head across a brook;
   Or by a cyder-press, with patient look,
     Thou watchest the last oozings hours by hours.

Where are the songs of Spring? Ay, where are they?
   Think not of them, thou hast thy music too, –
While barred clouds bloom the soft-dying day,
   And touch the stubble-plains with rosy hue;
Then in a wailful choir the small gnats mourn
   Among the river-sallows, borne aloft
     Or sinking as the light wind lives or dies;
And full-grown lambs loud bleat from hilly bourn;
   Hedge-crickets sing; and now with treble soft
   The red-breast whistles from a garden-croft;
     And gathering swallows twitter in the skies.

JOHN KEATS

From The Boat on the Serchio

Our boat is asleep on Serchio's stream,
Its sails are folded like thoughts in a dream,
The helm sways idly, hither and thither;
   Dominic, the boat-man, has brought the mast,
   And the oars and the sails; but 'tis sleeping fast,
Like a beast, unconscious of its tether.

The stars burnt out in the pale blue air,
And the thin white moon lay withering there,
To tower, and cavern, and rift and tree,
The owl and the bat fled drowsily.
Day had kindled the dewy woods,
  And the rocks above and the stream below,
And the vapours in their multitudes,
  And the Apennine shroud of summer snow,
And clothed with light of aëry gold
The mists in their eastern caves uprolled.

Day had awakened all things that be,
The lark and the thrush and the swallow free,
  And the milkmaid's song and the mower's scythe
And the matin-bell and the mountain bee:
Fire-flies were quenched on the dewy corn.
  Glow-worms went out on the river's brim,
  Like lamps which a student forgets to trim:
The beetle forgot to wind his horn,
  The crickets were still in the meadow and hill:
Like a flock of rooks at a farmer's gun
Night's dreams and terrors, every one,
Fled from the brains which are their prey
From the lamp's death to the morning ray. . . .

'What think you, as she lies in her green cove,
Our little sleeping boat is dreaming of?'
'If morning dreams are true, why I should guess
That she was dreaming of our idleness,
And of the miles of watery way
We should have led her by this time of day.' –

'Never mind,' said Lionel,
'Give care to the winds, they can bear it well
About yon poplar tops; and see
The white clouds are driving merrily,
And the stars we miss this morn will light
More willingly our return to-night. –
How it whistles, Dominic's long black hair!
List my dear fellow; the breeze blows fair:
Hear how it sings into the air.'

'Of us and of our lazy motions,'
        Impatiently said Melchior,
'If I can guess a boat's emotions;
        And how we ought, two hours before.
To have been the devil knows where. . . .
    She dreams that we are not yet out of bed;
We'll put a soul into her, and a heart
Which like a dove chased by a dove shall beat.'
        .   .   .   .   .

        'Ay, heave the ballast overboard,
    And stow the eatables in the aft locker.'
'Would not this keg be best a little lowered?'
'No, now all's right.' 'Those bottles of warm tea –
(Give me some straw) – must be stowed tenderly;
Such as we used, in summer after six,
To cram in great-coat pockets, and to mix
Hard eggs and radishes and rolls at Eton,
And, couched on stolen hay in those green harbours
Farmers called gaps, and we schoolboys called arbours,
Would feast till eight.'
        .   .   .   .   .

        With a bottle in one hand,
As if his very soul were at a stand,
Lionel stood – when Melchior brought him steady: –
'Sit at the helm – fasten this sheet – all ready!' . . .

[100]

The Serchio, twisting forth
Between the marble barriers which it clove
   At Ripafratta, leads through the dread chasm
The wave that died the death which lovers love,
   Living in what it sought; as if this spasm
Had not yet past, the toppling mountains cling,
   But the clear stream in full enthusiasm
Pours itself on the plain, then wandering
   Down one clear path of effluence crystalline,
Sends its superfluous waves, that they may fling
   At Arno's feet tribute of corn and wine,
Then, through the pestilential deserts wild
   Of tangled marsh and woods of stunted pine,
It rushes to the Ocean.

PERCY BYSSHE SHELLEY

The Wind Tapped like a Tired Man

The Wind – tapped like a tired Man –
And like a Host – 'Come in'
I boldly answered – entered then
My Residence within

A Rapid – footless Guest –
To offer whom a Chair
Were as impossible as hand
A Sofa to the Air –

No Bone had He to bind Him –
His Speech was like the Push
Of numerous Humming Birds at once
From a superior Bush –

His Countenance – a Billow –
His Fingers, as He passed
Let go a music – as of tunes
Blown tremulous in Glass –

He visited – still flitting –
Then like a timid Man
Again, He tapped – 'twas flurriedly –
And I became alone –

EMILY DICKINSON

A View from Middle-Earth

This was my dream: Nature stood nigh me,
Said, 'Come with me, William, and view the world's
    wonders.'
To a mountain we moved – Middle-Earth its name is –
To learn by looking. With new sight I witnessed
The sun and the sea and the sand beside it,
And the secret places of grove and grassland
Where birds and beasts could mate unmolested –
The wildwood creatures, a blaze of beauty!
The wings of the wildfowl, so flecked with colours.
I saw man and his mate too, now poor, now with plenty,
In war and in peace – but where was their wisdom?
Grasping and greedy, they gave away nothing.

But the creatures followed the rule of Reason
Wise in their feeding and in their engendering.
No hound, nor horse, not one kind of creature,
Meddled with mate that was carrying young ones.
I watched the birds build nests in the bushes;
No human hand could have worked such weaving.
Where could we match the magpie's mastery
In twining twigs for the nest she'll breed in?
No carpenter could contrive such craftwork
No builder build it, whatever the blueprint.
Other birds were as much a marvel.
Some hid their homes from harm and hunters
In moor and marshes where men could not mark them,
Their eggs close hidden from foraging fingers.
Some in the tree-tops met and mated,
High out of harm when they hatched their young ones.
How did they know? What teacher taught them?
Then I stared at the sea, at the sky full of starlight,
At the flowers in the forest, their fresh fair colours,
At the grasses, even their green so varied,
Some grasses sweet, some sour to the tasting –
Too many the mysteries; but what most moved me
Was how Reason guided the whole of nature,
All creation, save one kind only –
Man and his mate.

WILLIAM LANGLAND
from *The Vision of Piers Plowman*
translated into modern English by Naomi Lewis

The Joy of Fishes

Chuang Tzu and Hui Tzu
Were crossing Hoa river
By the dam.

Chuang said:
'See how free
The fishes leap and dart:
That is their happiness.'

Hui replied:
'Since you are not a fish
How do you know
What makes fishes happy?'

Chuang said:
'Since you are not I
How can you possibly know
That I do not know
What makes fishes happy?'

Hui argued:
'If I, not being you,
Cannot know what you know
It follows that you
Not being a fish
Cannot know what they know.'

Chuang said:
'Wait a minute!
Let us get back
To the original question.

What you asked me was
"How do you know
What makes fishes happy?"
From the terms of your question
You evidently know I know
What makes fishes happy.

'I know the joy of fishes
In the river
Through my own joy, as I go walking
Along the same river.'

CHUANG TZU
translated by Thomas Merton

A Bird Came Down the Walk

A Bird came down the Walk –
He did not know I saw –
He bit an Angleworm in halves
And ate the fellow, raw,

And then he drank a Dew
From a convenient Grass –
And then hopped sidewise to the Wall
To let a Beetle pass –

He glanced with rapid eyes
That hurried all around –
They looked like frightened Beads, I thought –
He stirred his Velvet Head

Like one in danger, Cautious,
I offered him a Crumb
And he unrolled his feathers
And rowed him softer home –

[105]

Than Oars divide the Ocean,
Too silver for a seam –
Or Butterflies, off Banks of Noon
Leap, plashless as they swim.

EMILY DICKINSON

The Nightjar

We loved our Nightjar, but she would not stay with us.
We had found her lying as dead, but soft and warm,
Under the apple tree beside the old thatched wall.
Two days we kept her in a basket by the fire,
Fed her, and thought she well might live – till suddenly
In the very moment of most confiding hope
She raised herself all tense, quivered and drooped and died.
Tears sprang into my eyes – why not? the heart of man
Soon sets itself to love a living companion,
The more so if by chance it asks some care of him.
And this one had the kind of loveliness that goes
Far deeper than the optic nerve – full fathom five
To the soul's ocean cave, where Wonder and Reason
Tell their alternate dreams of how the world was made.
So wonderful she was – her wings the wings of night
But powdered here and there with tiny golden clouds
And wave-line markings like sea-ripples on the sand.
O how I wish I might never forget that bird –
Never!
        But even now, like all beauty of earth,
She is fading from me into the dusk of Time.

SIR HENRY NEWBOLT

Frutta di Mare

I am a sea-shell flung
Up from the ancient sea;
Now I lie here, among
Roots of a tamarisk tree;
No one listens to me.

I sing to myself all day
In a husky voice, quite low,
Things the great fishes say
And you must need to know;
All night I sing just so.

But lift me from the ground,
And hearken at my rim,
Only your sorrow's sound
Amazed, perplexed and dim,
Comes coiling to the brim;

For what the wise whales ponder
Awaking out from sleep,
The key to all your wonder,
The answers of the deep,
These to myself I keep.

GEOFFREY SCOTT

The Trees

The trees are coming into leaf
Like something almost being said;
The recent buds relax and spread,
Their greenness is a kind of grief.

Is it that they are born again
And we grow old? No, they die too.
Their yearly trick of looking new
Is written down in rings of grain.

Yet still the unresting castles thresh
In fullgrown thickness every May.
Last year is dead, they seem to say,
Begin afresh, afresh, afresh.

PHILIP LARKIN

Noises in the Night

Midnight's bell goes ting, ting, ting, ting, ting,
Then dogs do howl, and not a bird does sing
But the nightingale, and she goes twit, twit, twit.
Owls then on every bough do sit,
Ravens croak on chimney tops,
The cricket in the chamber hops,
And the cats cry mew, mew, mew.
The nibbling mouse is not asleep,
But he goes peep, peep, peep, peep.
   And the cats cry mew, mew, mew,
   And still the cats cry mew, mew, mew.

THOMAS MIDDLETON

Binsey Poplars
felled 1879

My aspens dear, whose airy cages quelled,
Quelled or quenched in leaves the leaping sun,
All felled, felled, are all felled;
   Of a fresh and following folded rank
        Not spared, not one
        That dandled a sandalled
    Shadow that swam or sank
On meadow and river and wind-wandering weed-winding
   bank.

  O if we but knew what we do
      When we delve or hew –
  Hack and rack the growing green!
     Since country is so tender
  To touch, her being só slender,
  That, like this sleek and seeing ball
  But a prick will make no eye at all,
  Where we, even where we mean
      To mend her we end her,
    When we hew or delve:
After-comers cannot guess the beauty been.
  Ten or twelve, only ten or twelve
    Strokes of havoc únselve
     The sweet especial scene,
   Rural scene, a rural scene,
   Sweet especial rural scene.

GERARD MANLEY HOPKINS

The destruction of trees always affected Hopkins. A diary note for April 1873 runs:

April 8 The ashtree growing in the corner of the garden was felled. It was lopped first: I heard the sound and looking out and seeing it maimed there came at that moment a great pang and I wished to die and not to see the inscapes of the world destroyed any more.

Binsey poplars were felled in Oxford in March 1879.

Bess My Badger

Bess my badger grew up
In a petshop in Leicester. Moony mask
Behind mesh. Dim eyes
Baffled by people. Customers cuddled her,

Tickled her belly, tamed her – her wildness
Got no exercise. Her power-tools,
Her miniature grizzly-bear feet,
Feet like garden-forks, had to be satisfied

Being just feet,
Trudging to-fro, to-fro, in her tight cage,
Her nose brushed by the mesh, this way, that way,
All night, every night, keeping pace

With the badgers out in the woods. She was
Learning to be a prisoner. She was perfecting
Being a prisoner. She was a prisoner. Till a girl
Bought her, to free her, and sold her to me.

What's the opposite of taming? I'm unteaching
Her tameness. First, I shut her in a stable.

But she liked being tame. That night, as every night,
At a bare patch of wall the length of her cage
To-fro, to-fro, she wore at the wood with her nose,
Practising her prison shuffle, her jail walk.

All day, dozing in the gloom, she waited for me.
Every supper-time, all she wanted was
Me to be a badger, and romp with her in the straw.
She laughed – a chuckling sort of snarl, a rattle,

And grabbed my toe in my shoe, and held it, hard,
Then rolled on to her back to be tickled.
'Be wild,' I told her. 'Be a proper badger.'
She twisted on to her feet, as if she agreed

And listened. Her head lifted – like a hand
Shaped to cast a snake's head shadow on the wall –
What she'd heard was a car. She waddled away
Shawled in her trailing cape of grey feathers,

And looked back. Sniffed a corner. Listened.

I could see she was lonely.

        A few nights later
Her claws went wild. And they tunnelled
From stable to stable, connecting four stables.

Then bored up through the wall so the long loft
Became her look-out. After that,
If shouting in the yard, or a tractor, disturbed her,
You'd see her peering down through the dusty panes,

And if the loft door had been blown open
She'd poke her face out, furious, then slam it.
Soon she'd quarried out through the back of the stables
And with about three cartloads of stony rubble

From under the stables, she landscaped her porchway –
And the world was hers. Now, nightly,
Whatever she can shift, she'll shift, or topple,
For the worm, the beetle, or the woodlouse beneath it.

She tasted clematis roots, and now she's an addict.
She corkscrews holes in the wet lawn with her nose,
Nipping out the lobworms. With her mine-detector
Finds all the flower-bulbs. Early workmen meet her

Plodding, bowlegged, home through the village.

[111]

Already she hardly needs me. Will she forget me?
Sometimes I leave black-treacle sandwiches,
A treat at her entrance, just to remind her –
She's our houseproud lodger, deepening her rooms.

Or are we her lodgers? To her
Our farm-buildings are her wild jumble of caves,
Infested by big monkeys. And she puts up with us –
Big noisy monkeys, addicted to diesel and daylight.

TED HUGHES

Parakeet

They always put a large crimson sheet
over his cage in the corner at night
because they said that our old parakeet
could not go to sleep in the lamplight.

Father bought him in a pub, not from a pet shop,
was told he would talk to us all day
but after a while it all came to a stop
and not a single word did he ever say

even when I called out 'Pretty Polly' and things like that,
cleaned out his home, looked after his feeds,
praised him when he turned into an acrobat,
rewarded him with apple cores and sunflower seeds.

On the morning of the winter day he died
I gave him some water and a handful of split peas
and then turning his blue and green head on one side
said very clearly 'Time, gentlemen, please.'

And toppled over from his perch on to the sand,
sharp eyes dulled, long feathers fading and still;
he had gone back to his South American land
to fly with his dazzle between green valley and hill.

Monkeys

Two little creatures
With faces the size of
A pair of pennies
Are clasping each other.
'Ah, do not leave me,'
One says to the other,
In the high monkey-
Cage in the beast-shop.

There are no people
To gape at them now,
For people are loth to
Peer in the dimness;
Have they not builded
Streets and playhouses,
Sky-signs and bars,
To lose the loneliness
Shaking the hearts
Of the two little Monkeys?

Yes. But who watches
The penny-small faces
Can hear the voices:
'Ah, do not leave me;

[113]

Suck I will give you,
Warmth and clasping,
And if you slip from
This beam I can never
Find you again.'

Dim is the evening,
And chill is the weather;
There, drawn from their coloured
Hemisphere,
The apes lilliputian
With faces the size of
A pair of pennies,
And voices as low as
The flow of my blood.

PADRAIC COLUM

Rose and Cushie

The cow low'd sadly o'er the distant gate,
In the mid field, and round our garden rail:
But naught her restless sorrow could abate,
Nor patting hands, nor clink of milking pail;
For she had lost the love she least could spare,
Her little suckling calf, her life of life,
In some far shambles waited for the knife,
And spent his sweet breath on the murderous air.
One single yearning sound, repeated still,
Moan'd from the croft, and wander'd down the hill:

[114]

The heedless train ran brawling down the line
On went the horseman and the market cart:
But little Rose, who loved the sheep and kine,
Ran home to tell of Cushie's broken heart.

CHARLES TENNYSON TURNER

Nell

Nellie Rakerfield
Came from an estate in Scotland,
Two years old, and won a championship.
It was not her fault that her foals
Were few, and mostly died or were runted.
She worked every day when she raised them,
Never was tired of dragging her
Nineteen hundred pounds
About the farm and the roads, with
Great loads behind it.
She never kicked, bit, nor crowded
In the stall,
Was always ready at a chirp
And seemed to have forgotten delicate care.

But the day they hitched her
To the corpse of her six-months-old colt,
She tried to run away, half way to the bush.
She never seemed quite so willing, afterward.
But the colt was too heavy.

RAYMOND KNISTER

Cats Crept Up on Me Slowly

Cats crept up on me slowly
as a child it was dogs and teachers
that allowed no privacy
now the persuasion of cats
keeps me busy
interpreting their differing
ways of asking questions.

URSULA LAIRD

The Wolf said to Francis

The wolf said to Francis
'You have more sense than some.
I will not spoil the legend;
Call me, and I shall come.

But in the matter of taming
Should you not look more near?
Those howlings come from humans.
Their hatred is their fear.

We are an orderly people.
Though great our pain and need,
We do not kill for torture;
We do not hoard for greed.

But the victim has the vision –
A gift of sorts that's given
As some might say, by history
And you, perhaps, by heaven.

[116]

Tomorrow or soon after
(Count centuries for days)
I see (and you may also
If you will turn your gaze) –

How the sons of man have taken
A hundredfold their share.
But the child of God, the creature,
Can rest his head nowhere.

See, sky and ocean empty,
The earth scorched to the bone;
By poison, gun, starvation
The last free creature gone.
But the swollen tide of humans
Sweeps on and on and on.

No tree, no bird, no grassland
Only increasing man,
And the prisoned beasts he feeds on –
Was *this* the heavenly plan?'

Francis stood there silent.
Francis bowed his head.
Clearly passed before him
All that the wolf had said.

Francis looked at his brother
He looked at the forest floor.
The vision pierced his thinking,
And with it, something more
That humans are stony listeners.

The legend stands as before.

A. G. ROCHELLE

The Turkish Trench Dog

Night held me as I crawled and scrambled near
The Turkish lines. Above, the mocking stars
Silvered the curving parapet, and clear
Cloud-latticed beams o'erflecked the land with bars;
I, crouching, lay between
Tense-listening armies, peering through the night,
Twin giants bound by tentacles unseen.
Here in dim-shadowed light
I saw him, as a sudden movement turned
His eyes toward me, glowing eyes that burned
A moment ere his snuffling muzzle found
My trail; and then as serpents mesmerize
He chained me with those unrelenting eyes,
That muscle-sliding rhythm, knit and bound
In spare-limbed symmetry, those perfect jaws
And soft approaching pitter-patter paws.
Nearer and nearer like a wolf he crept –
That moment had my swift revolver leapt –
But terror seized me, terror born of shame
Brought flooding revelation. For he came
As one who offers comradeship deserved,
An open ally of the human race,
And sniffing at my prostrate form unnerved
He licked my face.

GEOFFREY DEARMER

Mountain Lion

Climbing through the January snow, into the Lobo canyon
Dark grow the spruce-trees, blue is the balsam, water
    sounds still unfrozen, and the trail is still evident.

Men!
Two men!
Men! The only animal in the world to fear!

They hesitate.
We hesitate.
They have a gun.
We have no gun.

Then we all advance, to meet.

Two Mexicans, strangers, emerging out of the dark and
    snow and inwardness of the Lobo valley.
What are they doing here on this vanishing trail?

What is he carrying?
Something yellow.
A deer?

Qué tiene, amigo?
León –

He smiles, foolishly, as if he were caught doing wrong.
And we smile, foolishly, as if we didn't know.
He is quite gentle and dark-faced.

It is a mountain lion,
A long, long slim cat, yellow like a lioness.
Dead.

He trapped her this morning, he says, smiling foolishly.
Lift up her face,
Her round, bright face, bright as frost.
Her round, fine-fashioned head, with two dead ears;

And stripes in the brilliant frost of her face, sharp, fine dark
    rays,
Dark, keen, fine rays in the brilliant frost of her face.
Beautiful dead eyes.

Hermoso es!

They go out towards the open;
We go on into the gloom of Lobo.
And above the trees I found her lair,
A hole in the blood-orange brilliant rocks that stick up, a
    little cave.
And bones, and twigs, and a perilous ascent.

So, she will never leap up that way again, with the yellow
    flash of a mountain lion's long shoot!
And her bright striped frost-face will never watch any more,
    out of the shadow of the cave in the blood-orange rock,
Above the trees of the Lobo dark valley-mouth!

Instead, I look out.
And out to the dim of the desert, like a dream, never real;
To the snow of the Sangre de Cristo mountains, the ice of
    the mountains of Picoris,
And near across the opposite steep of snow, green trees
    motionless standing in snow, like a Christmas toy.

And I think in this empty world there was room for me and a
    mountain lion.
And I think in the world beyond, how easily we might spare
    a million or two of humans
And never miss them.
Yet what a gap in the world, the missing white frost-face of
    that slim yellow mountain lion!

D. H. LAWRENCE

The Tyger

Tyger! Tyger! burning bright
In the forests of the night,
What immortal hand or eye
Could frame thy fearful symmetry?

In what distant deeps or skies
Burnt the fire of thine eyes?
On what wings dare he aspire?
What the hand dare seize the fire?

And what shoulder, and what art,
Could twist the sinews of thy heart?
And when thy heart began to beat,
What dread hand? and what dread feet?

What the hammer? what the chain?
In what furnace was thy brain?
What the anvil? what dread grasp
Dare its deadly terrors clasp?

When the stars threw down their spears,
And watered heaven with their tears,
Did he smile his work to see?
Did he who made the Lamb make thee?

Tyger! Tyger! burning bright
In the forests of the night,
What immortal hand or eye,
Dare frame thy fearful symmetry?

WILLIAM BLAKE

Elegy

My prime of youth is but a frost of cares,
  My feast of joy is but a dish of pain,
My crop of corn is but a field of tares,
  And all my good is but vain hope of gain;
    The day is past, and yet I saw no sun,
    And now I live, and now my life is done.

My tale was heard and yet it was not told,
  My fruit is fallen and yet my leaves are green,
My youth is spent and yet I am not old,
  I saw the world and yet I was not seen;
    My thread is cut and yet it is not spun,
    And now I live, and now my life is done.

I sought my death and found it in my womb,
  I looked for life and saw it was a shade,
I trod the earth and knew it was my tomb,
  And now I die, and now I was but made;
    My glass is full, and now my glass is run,
    And now I live, and now my life is done.

CHIDIOCK TICHBORNE

How Should I Your True Love Know

How should I your true love know
   From another one?
By his cockle hat and staff,
   And his sandal shoon.

He is dead and gone, lady,
   He is dead and gone;
At his head a grass-green turf,
   At his heels a stone.

White his shroud as the mountain snow,
   Larded with sweet flowers;
Which bewept to the grave did not go
   With true-love showers.

WILLIAM SHAKESPEARE
from *Hamlet*

In Plague Time

Adieu, farewell earth's bliss,
This world uncertain is;
Fond are life's lustful joys,
Death proves them all but toys,
None from his darts can fly.
I am sick, I must die.
   Lord, have mercy on us!

Rich men, trust not in wealth,
Gold cannot buy you health;
Physic himself must fade,
All things to end are made.
The plague full swift goes by.
I am sick, I must die.
   Lord, have mercy on us!

Beauty is but a flower
Which wrinkles will devour;
Brightness falls from the air,
Queens have died young and fair,
Dust hath closed Helen's eye.
I am sick, I must die.
   Lord, have mercy on us!

Strength stoops unto the grave,
Worms feed on Hector brave,
Swords may not fight with fate,
Earth still holds ope her gate.
Come! come! the bells do cry.
I am sick, I must die.
   Lord, have mercy on us!

Wit with his wantonness
Tasteth death's bitterness;
Hell's executioner
Hath no ears for to hear
What vain art can reply.
I am sick, I must die.
   Lord, have mercy on us!

Haste, therefore, each degree,
To welcome destiny.
Heaven is our heritage,
Earth but a player's stage;
Mount we unto the sky.
I am sick, I must die.
    Lord, have mercy on us!

THOMAS NASHE

Fear No More the Heat o' the Sun

Fear no more the heat o' the sun,
    Nor the furious winter's rages;
Thou thy worldly task hast done,
    Home art gone, and ta'en thy wages.
Golden lads and girls all must,
As chimney-sweepers, come to dust.

Fear no more the frown o' the great,
    Thou art past the tyrant's stroke;
Care no more to clothe and eat,
    To thee the reed is as the oak.
The sceptre, learning, physic, must
All follow this, and come to dust.

Fear no more the lightning-flash,
    Nor the all-dreaded thunder-stone;
Fear not slander, censure rash;
    Thou hast finished joy and moan.
All lovers young, all lovers must
Consign to thee, and come to dust.

WILLIAM SHAKESPEARE
from *Cymbeline*

Dirge in Cymbeline

To fair Fidele's grassy tomb
   Soft maids and village hinds shall bring
Each opening sweet of earliest bloom,
   And rifle all the breathing spring.

No wailing ghost shall dare appear
   To vex with shrieks this quiet grove;
But shepherd lads assemble here,
   And melting virgins own their love.

No withered witch shall here be seen;
   No goblins lead their nightly crew:
The female fays shall haunt the green,
   And dress thy grave with pearly dew.

The redbreast oft, at evening hours,
   Shall kindly lend his little aid,
With hoary moss, and gathered flowers,
   To deck the ground where thou art laid.

When howling winds, and beating rain,
   In tempests shake the sylvan cell;
Or midst the chase, on every plain,
   The tender thought on thee shall dwell;

Each lonely scene shall thee restore;
   For thee the tear be duly shed;
Beloved, till life can charm no more,
   And mourned till Pity's self be dead.

WILLIAM COLLINS

Lycidas

Yet once more, O ye laurels, and once more
Ye myrtles brown, with ivy never sere,
I come to pluck your berries harsh and crude,
And with forced fingers rude,
Shatter your leaves before the mellowing year.
Bitter constraint, and sad occasion dear,
Compels me to disturb your season due:
For Lycidas is dead, dead ere his prime
Young Lycidas, and hath not left his peer:
Who would not sing for Lycidas? he knew
Himself to sing, and build the lofty rhyme.
He must not float upon his watery bier
Unwept, and welter to the parching wind,
Without the meed of some melodious tear.
Begin then, Sisters of the sacred well,
That from beneath the seat of Jove doth spring,
Begin, and somewhat loudly sweep the string.
Hence with denial vain, and coy excuse,
So may some gentle Muse
With lucky words favour my destined urn,
And as he passes turn,
And bid fair peace to be my sable shroud.
For we were nursed upon the self-same hill,
Fed the same flock, by fountain, shade, and rill.
  Together both, ere the high lawns appeared
Under the opening eye-lids of the morn,
We drove afield, and both together heard
What time the gray-fly winds her sultry horn,
Battening our flocks with the fresh dews of night,
Oft till the star that rose at evening, bright
Towards heaven's descent had sloped his westering wheel.
Meanwhile the rural ditties were not mute,

Tempered to th' oaten flute,
Rough satyrs danced, and fauns with cloven heel,
From the glad sound would not be absent long,
And old Damœtas loved to hear our song.

But O the heavy change, now thou art gone,
Now thou art gone, and never must return!
Thee, shepherd, thee the woods and desert caves,
With wild thyme and the gadding vine o'ergrown,
And all their echoes mourn.
The willows, and the hazel copses green,
Shall now no more be seen,
Fanning their joyous leaves to thy soft lays.
As killing as the canker to the rose,
Or taint-worm to the weanling herds that graze,
Or frost to flowers, that their gay wardrobe wear,
When first the white thorn blows;
Such, Lycidas, thy loss to shepherd's ear.

Where were ye, nymphs, when the remorseless deep
Closed o'er the head of your loved Lycidas?
For neither were ye playing on the steep,
Where your old bards, the famous Druids, lie,
Nor on the shaggy top of Mona high,
Nor yet where Deva spreads her wizard stream:
Ay me, I fondly dream!
Had ye been there – for what could that have done?
What could the Muse herself that Orpheus bore,
The Muse herself, for her enchanting son
Whom universal Nature did lament,
When by the rout that made the hideous roar,
His gory visage down the stream was sent,
Down the swift Hebrus to the Lesbian shore?

Alas! What boots it with incessant care
To tend the homely slighted shepherd's trade,
And strictly meditate the thankless Muse?
Were it not better done as others use,

To sport with Amaryllis in the shade,
Or with the tangles of Neæra's hair?
Fame is the spur that the clear spirit doth raise
(That last infirmity of noble mind)
To scorn delights, and live laborious days;
But the fair guerdon when we hope to find,
And think to burst out into sudden blaze,
Comes the blind Fury with th' abhorrèd shears,
And slits the thin spun life. But not the praise,
Phoebus replied, and touched my trembling ears;
Fame is no plant that grows on mortal soil,
Nor in the glistering foil
Set off to th' world, nor in broad rumour lies,
But lives and spreads aloft by those pure eyes,
And perfect witness of all-judging Jove;
As He pronounces lastly on each deed,
Of so much fame in Heav'n expect thy meed.
  O fountain Arethuse, and thou honoured flood,
Smooth-sliding Mincius, crowned with vocal reeds,
That strain I heard was of a higher mood:
But now my oat proceeds,
And listens to the herald of the sea,
That came in Neptune's plea.
He asked the waves, and asked the felon winds,
What hard mishap hath doomed this gentle swain?
And questioned every gust of rugged wings
That blows from off each beakèd promontory.
They knew not of his story,
And sage Hippotades their answer brings,
That not a blast was from his dungeon strayed,
The air was calm, and on the level brine
Sleek Panope with all her sisters played.
It was that fatal and perfidious bark
Built in th' eclipse, and rigged with curses dark,
That sunk so low that sacred head of thine.

[130]

Next Camus, reverend sire, went footing slow,
His mantle hairy, and his bonnet sedge,
Inwrought with figures dim, and on the edge
Like to that sanguine flower inscribed with woe.
Ah! Who hath reft (quoth he) my dearest pledge?
Last came, and last did go,
The pilot of the Galilean lake,
Two massy keys he bore of metals twain,
(The golden opes, the iron shuts amain)
He shook his mitred locks, and stern bespake:
How well could I have spared for thee, young swain,
Enow of such as for their belly's sake
Creep and intrude, and climb into the fold?
Of other care they little reckoning make,
Than how to scramble at the shearers' feast,
And shove away the worthy bidden guest.
Blind mouths! that scarce themselves know how to hold
A sheep-hook, or have learned aught else the least
That to the faithful herdman's art belongs!
What recks it them? What need they? They are sped;
And when they list, their lean and flashy songs
Grate on their scrannel pipes of wretched straw.
The hungry sheep look up, and are not fed,
But swoll'n with wind, and the rank mist they draw,
Rot inwardly, and foul contagion spread:
Beside what the grim wolf with privy paw
Daily devours apace, and nothing said,
But that two-handed engine at the door,
Stands ready to smite once, and smite no more.
    Return, Alpheus, the dread voice is past,
That shrunk thy streams; return, Sicilian Muse,
And call the vales, and bid them hither cast
Their bells and flow'rets of a thousand hues.
Ye valleys low, where the mild whispers use
Of shades and wanton winds and gushing brooks,

On whose fresh lap the swart star sparely looks,
Throw hither all your quaint enamelled eyes,
That on the green turf suck the honied showers.
And purple all the ground with vernal flowers.
Bring the rathe primrose that forsaken dies,
The tufted crow-toe, and pale jessamine,
The white pink, and the pansy freaked with jet,
The glowing violet,
The musk-rose, and the well-attired woodbine,
With cowslips wan that hang the pensive head,
And every flower that sad embroidery wears:
Bid Amaranthus all his beauty shed,
And daffadillies fill their cups with tears,
To strew the laureate hearse where Lycid lies.
For so to interpose a little ease,
Let our frail thoughts dally with false surmise.
Ay me! Whilst thee the shores and sounding seas
Wash far away, where'er thy bones are hurled,
Whether beyond the stormy Hebrides,
Where thou perhaps under the whelming tide
Visit'st the bottom of the monstrous world;
Or whether thou to our moist vows denied,
Sleep'st by the fable of Bellerus old,
Where the great vision of the guarded mount
Looks toward Namancos and Bayona's hold;
Look homeward, Angel, now, and melt with ruth,
And, O ye dolphins, waft the hapless youth.

   Weep no more, woeful shepherds, weep no more,
For Lycidas your sorrow is not dead,
Sunk through he be beneath the watery floor,
So sinks the day-star in the ocean bed,
And yet anon repairs his drooping head,
And tricks his beams, and with new spangled ore
Flames in the forehead of the morning sky:
So Lycidas sunk low, but mounted high,

Through the dear might of him that walked the waves,
Where other groves, and other streams along
With nectar pure his oozy locks he laves,
And hears the unexpressive nuptial song,
In the blest kingdoms meek of joy and love.
There entertain him all the saints above,
In solemn troops, and sweet societies
That sing, and singing in their glory move,
And wipe the tears for ever from his eyes.
Now Lycidas the shepherds weep no more;
Henceforth thou art the genius of the shore,
In thy large recompense, and shalt be good
To all that wander in that perilous flood.
    Thus sang the uncouth swain to th' oaks and rills.
While the still morn went out with sandals gray,
He touched the tender stops of various quills,
With eager thought warbling his Doric lay:
And now the sun had stretched out all the hills,
And now was dropped into the western bay;
At last he rose, and twitched his mantle blue:
To-morrow to fresh woods, and pastures new.

JOHN MILTON

From On the Death of Doctor Swift

The time is not remote when I
Must by the course of nature die; . . .
Behold the fatal day arrive!
'How is the dean?' 'He's just alive.'
Now the departing prayer is read.
'He hardly breathes.' 'The dean is dead.'

[133]

Before the passing bell begun,
The news through half the town is run.
'O! may we all for death prepare!
What has he left? and who's his heir?' . . .

My female friends, whose tender hearts
Have better learned to act their parts,
Receive the news in doleful dumps:
'The dean is dead – pray what is trumps? –
The Lord have mercy on his soul!
– Ladies, I'll venture for the vole. –
Six deans, they say, must bear the pall –
I wish I knew what king to call. –
Madam, your husband will attend
The funeral of so good a friend?
No, madam, 'tis a shocking sight,
And he's engaged to-morrow night;
My Lady Club will take it ill
If he should fail her at quadrille.
He loved the dean – I lead a heart –
But dearest friends, they say, must part.
His time was come, he ran his race;
We hope he's in a better place. . . .''

He gave the little wealth he had
To build a house for fools and mad;
And showed by one satiric touch
No nation wanted it so much.
That kingdom he had left his debtor,
I wish it soon may have a better.

JONATHAN SWIFT

Oh! Sing Unto My Roundelay

Oh! sing unto my roundelay;
  Oh! drop the briny tear with me;
Dance no more at holiday;
  Like a running river be.
    My love is dead,
Gone to his death-bed
    All under the willow-tree.

Black his hair as the winter night,
  White his rode[1] as the summer snow,
Red his face as the morning light;
  Cold he lies in the grave below.
    My love is dead
    Gone to his death-bed,
    All under the willow-tree.

Sweet his tongue as the throstle's note,
  Quick in dance as thought can be,
Deft his tabour, cudgel stout;
  Oh! he lies by the willow-tree.
    My love is dead,
    Gone to his death-bed,
    All under the willow-tree.

Hark! the raven flaps his wing,
  In the briared dell below;
Hark! the death-owl loud doth sing
  To the night-mares, as they go.
    My love is dead,
    Gone to his death-bed,
    All under the willow-tree.

[1]Skin

See! the white moon shines on high,
   Whiter is my true love's shroud,
Whiter than the morning sky,
   Whiter than the evening cloud.
     My love is dead,
     Gone to his death-bed,
     All under the willow-tree.

Here, upon my true love's grave,
   Shall the barren flowers be laid;
Not one holy saint to save
   All the celness[1] of a maid.
     My love is dead,
     Gone to his death-bed
     All under the willow-tree.

With my hands I'll dente[2] the briars,
   Round his holy corse to gre,[3]
Elfin fairy, light your fires,
   Here my body still shall be.
     My love is dead
     Gone to his death-bed,
     All under the willow-tree.

Come, with acorn-cup and thorn,
   Drain my hartys blood away;
Life and all its good I scorn,
   Dance by night, or feast by day.
     My love is dead,
     Gone to his death-bed,
     All under the willow-tree. . . .

THOMAS CHATTERTON
from *Aella*
See note on page 90

[1]coldness   [2]fasten   [3]grow

[136]

If One Should Bring Me this Report

If one should bring me this report,
   That thou hadst touch'd the land to-day,
   And I went down unto the quay,
And found thee lying in the port;

And standing, muffled round with woe,
   Should see thy passengers in rank
   Come stepping lightly down the plank,
And beckoning unto those they know;

And if along with these should come
   The man I held as half-divine;
   Should strike a sudden hand in mine,
And ask a thousand things of home;

And I should tell him all my pain,
   And how my life had droop'd of late
   And he should sorrow o'er my state
And marvel what possess'd my brain;

And I perceived no touch of change,
   No hint of death in all his frame,
   But found him all in all the same,
I should not feel it to be strange.

ALFRED LORD TENNYSON
from *In Memoriam*

A Slumber Did My Spirit Seal

A slumber did my spirit seal;
   I had no human fears:
She seem'd a thing that could not feel
   The touch of earthly years.

No motion has she now, no force;
   She neither hears nor sees;
Roll'd round in earth's diurnal course
   With rocks, and stones, and trees.

WILLIAM WORDSWORTH

From Thyrsis

*A Monody, to commemorate the author's friend, Arthur Hugh Clough,
who died at Florence, 1861*

How changed is here each spot man makes or fills!
   In the two Hinkseys nothing keeps the same;
     The village-street its haunted mansion lacks,
And from the sign is gone Sibylla's name,
     And from the roofs the twisted chimney-stacks;
      Are ye too changed, ye hills?
See, 'tis no foot of unfamiliar men
   To-night from Oxford up your pathway strays
   Here came I often, often, in old days;
Thyrsis and I; we still had Thyrsis then. . . .

Lovely all times she lies, lovely to-night!
   Only, methinks, some loss of habit's power
     Befalls me wandering through this upland dim;

Once pass'd I blindfold here, at any hour,
  Now seldom come I, since I came with him.
    That single elm-tree bright
Against the west – I miss it! is it gone?
  We prized it dearly; while it stood, we said,
  Our friend, the Scholar-Gipsy, was not dead;
While the tree lived, he in these fields lived on.

Too rare, too rare, grow now my visits here!
  But once I knew each field, each flower, each stick;
    And with the country-folk acquaintance made
By barn in threshing-time, by new-built rick.
  Here, too, our shepherd-pipes we first assay'd.
    Ah me! this many a year
My pipe is lost, my shepherd's-holiday!
  Needs must I lose them, needs with heavy heart
  Into the world and wave of men depart;
But Thyrsis of his own will went away.

It irk'd him to be here, he could not rest.
  He loved each simple joy the country yields,
    He loved his mates; but yet he could not keep,
For that a shadow lower'd on the fields,
  Here with the shepherds and the silly sheep.
    Some life of men unblest.
He knew, which made him droop, and fill'd his head.
  He went; his piping took a troubled sound
  Of storms that rage outside our happy ground;
He could not wait their passing, he is dead!

So, some tempestuous morn in early June,
  When the year's primal burst of bloom is o'er,
    Before the roses and the longest day –
When garden-walks, and all the grassy floor,
  With blossoms, red and white, of fallen May,
    And chestnut-flowers are strewn –

So have I heard the cuckoo's parting cry,
    From the wet field, through the vext garden-trees,
    Come with the volleying rain and tossing breeze:
The bloom is gone, and with the bloom go I.

Too quick despairer, wherefore wilt thou go?
    Soon will the high Midsummer pomps come on,
      Soon will the musk carnations break and swell,
    Soon shall we have gold-dusted snapdragon,
      Sweet-William with its homely cottage-smell,
        And stocks in fragrant blow;
    Roses that down the alleys shine afar,
      And open, jasmine-muffled lattices,
      And groups under the dreaming garden-trees,
    And the full moon, and the white evening-star. . . .

I know these slopes; who knows them if not I? –
    But many a dingle on the loved hill-side,
      With thorns once studded, old, white-blossom'd trees,
    Where thick the cowslips grew, and, far descried,
      High tower'd the spikes of purple orchises,
        Hath since our day put by
    The coronals of that forgotten time.
      Down each green bank hath gone the ploughboy's
        team,
      And only in the hidden brookside gleam
    Primroses, orphans of the flowery prime.

Where is the girl, who, by the boatman's door,
    Above the locks, above the boating throng,
      Unmoor'd our skiff, when, through the Wytham flats,
    Red loosestrife and blond meadow-sweet among,
      And darting swallows, and light water-gnats,
        We track'd the shy Thames shore?

Where are the mowers, who, as the tiny swell
    Of our boat passing heav'd the river-grass,
    Stood with suspended scythe to see us pass? –
They all are gone, and thou art gone as well. . . .

But hush! the upland hath a sudden loss
    Of quiet; – Look! adown the dusk hill-side,
        A troop of Oxford hunters going home,
    As in old days, jovial and talking, ride!
        From hunting with the Berkshire hounds they come –
            Quick, let me fly, and cross
    Into yon further field! – 'Tis done; and see,
        Back'd by the sunset, which doth glorify
        The orange and pale violet evening-sky,
    Bare on its lonely ridge, the Tree! the Tree! . . .

Too rare, too rare, grow now my visits here!
    'Mid city-noise, not, as with thee of yore,
        Thyrsis, in reach of sheep-bells is my home!
    Then through the great town's harsh, heart-wearying
            roar,
        Let in thy voice a whisper often come,
            To chase fatigue and fear:
    Why faintest thou? I wander'd till I died.
        Roam on! the light we sought is shining still.
        Dost thou ask proof? Our Tree yet crowns the hill,
    Our Scholar travels yet the loved hillside.

                                    MATTHEW ARNOLD

Because I Could Not Stop for Death

Because I could not stop for Death –
He kindly stopped for me –
The Carriage held but just Ourselves –
And Immortality.

We slowly drove – He knew no haste
And I had put away
My labor and my leisure too,
For His Civility –

We passed the School, where Children strove
At Recess – in the Ring –
We passed the Fields of Gazing Grain –
We passed the Setting Sun –

Or rather – He passed Us –
The Dews drew quivering and chill –
For only Gossamer, my Gown –
My Tippet – only Tulle –

We paused before a House that seemed
A Swelling of the Ground –
The Roof was scarcely visible –
The Cornice – in the Ground –

Since then – 'tis Centuries – and yet
Feels shorter than the Day
I first surmised the Horses' Heads
Were toward Eternity –

EMILY DICKINSON

By St Thomas Water

By St Thomas Water
Where the river is thin
We look for a jam-jar
To catch the quick fish in.
Through St Thomas Church-yard
Jessie and I ran
The day we took the jam-pot
Off the dead man.

On the scuffed tombstone
The grey flowers fell,
Cracked was the water,
Silent the shell.
The snake for an emblem
Swirled on the slab,
Across the beach of sky the sun
Crawled like a crab.

'If we walk,' said Jessie,
'Seven times round,
We shall hear a dead man
Speaking underground.'
Round the stone we danced, we sang,
Watched the sun drop,
Laid our hearts and listened
At the tomb-top.

Soft as the thunder
At the storm's start
I heard a voice as clear as blood,
Strong as the heart.
But what words were spoken
I can never say,
I shut my fingers round my head,
Drove them away.

'What are those letters, Jessie,
Cut so sharp and trim
All round this holy stone
With earth up to the brim?'
Jessie traced the letters
Black as coffin-lead.
'*He is not dead but sleeping,*'
Slowly she said.

I looked at Jessie,
Jessie looked at me,
And our eyes in wonder
Grew wide as the sea.
Past the green and bending stones
We fled hand in hand,
Silent through the tongues of grass
To the river strand.

By the creaking cypress
We moved as soft as smoke
For fear all the people
Underneath awoke.
Over all the sleepers
We darted light as snow
In case they opened up their eyes,
Called us from below.

Many a day has faltered
Into many a year
Since the dead awoke and spoke
And we would not hear.
Waiting in the cold grass
Under a crinkled bough,
Quiet stone, cautious stone,
What do you tell me now?

CHARLES CAUSLEY

Being Called For

Come in at the low-silled window,
Enter by the door through the vine-leaves
Growing over the lintel. I have hung bells at the
Window to be stirred by the breath of your
Coming, which may be at any season.

In winter the snow throws
Light on the ceiling. If you come in winter
There will be a blue shadow before you
Cast on the threshold.

In summer an eddying of white dust
And a brightness falling between the leaves.

When you come I am ready: only, uncertain –
Shall we be leaving at once on another journey?
I would like first to write it all down and leave the pages
On the table weighted with a stone,
Nevertheless I have put in a basket
The coins for the ferry.

ROSEMARY DOBSON

The Ambassador

Underneath the broad hat is the face of the Ambassador
He rides on a white horse through hell looking two ways.
Doors open before him and shut when he has passed.
He is master of the mysteries and in the market place.
He is known. He stole the trident, the girdle,
The sword, the sceptre and many mechanical instruments.
Thieves honour him. In the underworld he rides carelessly.
Sometimes he rises into the air and flies silently.

STEVIE SMITH

The Border

What shall avail me
When I reach the border?
This staff will fail me,
This pass all in order.

These wo_ds I have learned
Will not help me then,
These honours hard earned,
And applause of men.

My harp truly set
Will break string by string;
I shall quite forget
That once I could sing.

Absence pure and cold
Of sense and memory
Lightly will hold
All that is me.

All, all will fail me,
Tongue, foot and hand.
Strange I shall hale me
To that strange land.

EDWIN MUIR

Guest

Is the kitchen tap still dripping?
You should always chain the door at nights.
Soon the roof will need repairing.
What's happening these days at the office?
Too much coffee agitates the nerves.
Now don't forget to spray the roses.
Do see the doctor about those twinges.

But tell me where you are! How is it there?
Are you in pain or bliss? And what is bliss?
Are you lonely? Do we live for ever?
How do you pass the time, if time there is?
Does God exist? Is God loving?
Why must his ways be so mysterious?
Is there a purpose in our living

*

Why won't you speak of things that matter?
You used to be so wise, so serious.
Now all our talk is roofs and roses
Like neighbours chatting at the corner.

Here wisdom is as common as the air,
Great matters are the ground I tread.
Tell me, what weather are you having?
Are the planes still noisy overhead?
Ask my old mates how work is going –

Don't be angry, dear. This hasn't changed:
Those things we lack are what we covet.
I am the guest, the one to be indulged.

D. J. ENRIGHT

A Form of Epitaph

Name in block letters   *None that signified*
Purpose of visit   *Barely ascertained*
Reasons for persevering   *Hope – or pride*
Status before admission here   *Regained*
Previous experience   *Nil, or records lost*
Requirements   *Few in fact, not all unmet*
Knowledge accumulated   *At a cost*
Plans   *Vague*   Sworn declaration   *Not in debt*

Evidence of departure   *Orthodox*
Country of origin   *Stateless then, as now*
Securities where held   *In one wood box*
Address for future reference   *Below*

Is further time desired?   *Not the clock's*
Was permit of return petitioned?   *No*

LAWRENCE WHISTLER

Pied à Terre

A *pied à terre*?
That may well be what the Dead
Call our earthly life.

ANNE BLOCH

(*Haiku*)

'A Host of Furious Fancies'

Tom o' Bedlam's Song

From the hag and hungry goblin
That into rags would rend ye
And the spirit that stands by the naked man
In the Book of Moons defend ye!
That of your five sound senses
You never be forsaken
Nor wander from your selves with Tom
Abroad to beg your bacon.
   While I do sing 'Any food, any feeding,
   Feeding, drink or clothing.'
   Come dame or maid, be not afraid,
   Poor Tom will injure nothing . . .

With a thought I took for Maudlin
And a cruse of cockle pottage,
With a thing thus tall, sky bless you all,
I befell into this dotage.
I slept not since the Conquest,
Till then I never wakèd
Till the roguish boy of love where I lay
Me found and stripped me naked.
   And now I sing 'Any food, any feeding,
   Feeding, drink or clothing.'
   Come dame or maid, be not afraid,
   Poor Tom will injure nothing . . .

When I short have shorn my sour face
And swigged my horny barrel
In an oaken inn I pound my skin
As a suit of gilt apparel.
The moon's my constant Mistress
And the lowly owl my marrow;
The flaming Drake and the Nightcrow make
Me music to my sorrow.
　　While I do sing 'Any food, any feeding,
　　Feeding, drink or clothing.'
　　Come dame or maid, be not afraid,
　　Poor Tom will injure nothing . . .

I know more than Apollo,
For oft when he lies sleeping
I see the stars at bloody wars
In the wounded welkin weeping,
The moon embrace her shepherd
And the queen of Love her warrior,
While the first doth horn the star of morn
And the next the heavenly Farrier,
　　While I do sing 'Any food, any feeding,
　　Feeding, drink or clothing.'
　　Come dame or maid, be not afraid,
　　Poor Tom will injure nothing.

With an host of furious fancies
Whereof I am commander,
With a burning spear, and a horse of air,
To the wilderness I wander.
By a knight of ghosts and shadows
I summoned am to tourney
Ten leagues beyond the wide world's end.
Methinks it is no journey.

Yet will I sing 'Any food, any feeding,
Feeding, drink or clothing.'
Come dame or maid, be not afraid,
Poor Tom will injure nothing.

ANON

This Palace Standeth in the Air

This palace standeth in the air,
By necromancy placèd there,
That it no tempest needs to fear,
    Which way soe'er it blow it.
And somewhat southward towards the noon,
Whence lies a way up to the moon,
And thence the Fairy can as soon
    Pass to the earth below it. . . .

MICHAEL DRAYTON
from *The Fairy Palace*

On Leaping Over the Moon

I saw new Worlds beneath the Water lie,
    New People; yea, another Sky
        And Sun, which seen by Day
        Might things more clear display.
            Just such another
            Of late my Brother

Did in his Travel see, and saw by Night,
    A much more strange and wondrous Sight:
Nor could the World exhibit such another,
    So Great a Sight, but in a Brother.

Adventure strange! No such in Story we,
    New or old, true or feigned, see.
        On Earth he seem'd to move
        Yet Heaven went above;
            Up in the Skies
            His body flies
In open, visible, yet Magic, sort:
    As he along the Way did sport,
Over the Flood he takes his nimble Course
    Without the help of feigned Horse.

As he went tripping o'er the King's high-way,
    A little pearly river lay
        O'er which, without a wing
        Or Oar, he dar'd to swim,
            Swim through the air
            On body fair;
He would not use nor trust *Icarian* wings
    Lest they should prove deceitful things;
For had he fall'n, it had been wondrous high,
    Not from, but from above, the sky:

He might have dropt through that thin element
    Into a fathomless descent;
        Unto the nether sky
        That did beneath him lie,
            And there might tell
            What wonders dwell
On earth above. Yet doth he briskly run,
    And bold the danger overcome;

[154]

Who, as he leapt, with joy related soon
    How *happy* he o'er-leapt the Moon.

What wondrous things upon the Earth are done
    Beneath, and yet above the sun?
        Deeds all appear again
        In higher spheres; remain
            In clouds as yet:
            But there they get
Another light, and in another way
    Themselves to us *above* display.
The skies themselves this earthly globe surround;
    W'are even here within them found.

On heav'nly ground within the skies we walk,
    And in this middle centre talk:
        Did we but wisely move,
        On earth in heav'n above,
            Then soon should we
            Exalted be
Above the sky: from whence whoever falls,
    Through a long dismal precipice,
Sinks to the deep abyss where *Satan* crawls
    Where horrid Death and Despair lies.

As much as others thought themselves to lie
Beneath the moon, so much more high
    Himself he thought to fly
    Above the starry sky,
        As *that* he spied
        Below the tide.
Thus did he yield me in the shady night
    A wondrous and instructive light,
Which taught me that under our feet there is,
    As o'er our heads, a place of bliss.

[155]

To the same purpose; he, not long before
   Brought home from nurse, going to the door
     To do some little thing
     He must not do within,
       With wonder cries,
       As in the skies
He saw the moon, *O yonder is the moon*
   Newly come after me to town,
That shin'd at Lugwardin but yesternight,
   Where I enjoy'd the self-same light.

As if it had ev'n twenty thousand faces,
   It shines at once in many places;
     To all the earth so wide
     God doth the stars divide
       With so much art
       The moon impart,
They serve us all; serve wholly ev'ry one
   As if they served him alone.
While every single person hath such store,
   'Tis want of sense that makes us poor.

THOMAS TRAHERNE

Fafnir and the Knights

     In the quiet waters
     Of the forest pool
     Fafnir the dragon
     His tongue will cool

His tongue will cool
And his muzzle dip
Until the soft waters lave
His muzzle tip

Happy simple creature
In his coat of mail
With a mild bright eye
And a waving tail

Happy the dragon
In the days expended
Before the time had come for dragons
To be hounded

Delivered in their simplicity
To the Knights of the Advancing Band
Who seeing the simple dragon
Must kill him out of hand

The time has not come yet
But must come soon
Meanwhile happy Fafnir
Take thy rest in the afternoon

Take thy rest
Fafnir while thou mayest
In the green grass
Where thou liest

Happy knowing not
In thy simplicity
That the knights have come
To do away with thee.

When thy body shall be torn
And thy lofty spirit
Broken into pieces
For a knight's merit

When thy lifeblood shall be spilt
And thy Being mild
In torment and dismay
To death beguiled

Fafnir, I shall say then,
Thou art better dead
For the knights have burnt thy grass
And thou couldst not have fed.

STEVIE SMITH

Overheard on a Saltmarsh

Nymph, nymph, what are your beads?

Green glass, goblin.   Why do you stare at them?

Give them me.

        No.

Give them me.   Give them me.

                No.

Then I will howl all night in the reeds,
Lie in the mud and howl for them.

Goblin, why do you love them so?

They are better than stars or water,
Better than voices of winds that sing,
Better than any man's fair daughter,
Your green glass beads on a silver ring.

Hush, I stole them out of the moon.

Give me your beads, I want them.

                              No.

I will howl in a deep lagoon
For your green glass beads, I love them so.
Give them me.   Give them.

                         No.

HAROLD MONRO

Peak and Puke

From his cradle in the glamourie
They have stolen my wee brother,
Housed a changeling in his swaddlings
For to fret my own poor mother.
Pules it in the candle light
Wi' a cheek so lean and white,
Chinkling up its eyne so wee
Wailing shrill at her an' me.
It we'll neither rock nor tend
Till the Silent Silent send,
Lapping in their waesome arms
Him they stole with spells and charms,
Till they take this changeling creature
Back to its own fairy nature –
Cry! Cry! as long as may be,
Ye shall ne'er be woman's baby!

WALTER DE LA MARE

The Frog Prince

I am a frog
I live under a spell
I live at the bottom
Of a green well

And here I must wait
Until a maiden places me
On her royal pillow
And kisses me
In her father's palace.

The story is familiar
Everybody knows it well
But do other enchanted people feel as nervous
As I do? The stories do not tell,

Ask if they will be happier
When the changes come
As already they are fairly happy
In a frog's doom?

I have been a frog now
For a hundred years
And in all this time
I have not shed many tears,

I am happy, I like the life,
Can swim for many a mile
(When I have hopped to the river)
And am for ever agile.

And the quietness,
Yes, I like to be quiet
I am habituated
To a quiet life,

But always when I think these thoughts
As I sit in my well
Another thought comes to me and says:
It is part of the spell

To be happy
To work up contentment
To make much of being a frog
To fear disenchantment

Says, It will be *heavenly*
To be set free,
Cries, *Heavenly* the girl who disenchants
And the royal times, *heavenly*,
And I think it will be.

Come then, royal girl and royal times,
Come quickly,
I can be happy until you come
But I cannot be heavenly,
Only disenchanted people
Can be heavenly.

STEVIE SMITH

The Fairies

Up the airy mountain,
   Down the rushy glen,
We daren't go a-hunting
   For fear of little men;
Wee folk, good folk,
   Trooping all together;
Green jacket, red cap,
   And white owl's feather!

Down along the rocky shore
   Some make their home,
They live on crispy pancakes
   Of yellow tide-foam;
Some in the reeds
   Of the black mountain-lake,
With frogs for their watch-dogs,
   All night awake.

High on the hill-top
   The old King sits;
He is now so old and gray
   He's nigh lost his wits.
With a bridge of white mist
   Columbkill he crosses,
On his stately journeys
   From Slieveleague to Rosses;
Or going up with music
   On cold starry nights,
To sup with the Queen
   Of the gay Northern Lights.

They stole little Bridget
   For seven years long;
When she came down again
   Her friends were all gone.
They took her lightly back,
   Between the night and morrow,
They thought that she was fast asleep,
   But she was dead with sorrow.
They have kept her ever since
   Deep within the lake,
On a bed of flag-leaves,
   Watching till she wake.

By the craggy hill-side,
   Through the mosses bare,
They have planted thorn-trees
   For pleasure here and there.
Is any man so daring
   As to dig one up in spite,
He shall find the thornies set
   In his bed at night.

Up the airy mountain,
   Down the rushy glen,
We daren't go a-hunting
   For fear of little men;
Wee folk, good folk,
   Trooping all together;
Green jacket, red cap,
   And white owl's feather!

WILLIAM ALLINGHAM

Prognosis

Goodbye, Winter,
The days are getting longer,
The tea-leaf in the teacup
Is herald of a stranger.

Will he bring me business
Or will he bring me gladness
Or will he come for cure
Of his own sickness?

With a pedlar's burden
Walking up the garden
Will he come to beg
Or will he come to bargain?

Will he come to pester,
To cringe or to bluster,
A promise in his palm
Or a gun in his holster?

Will his name be John
Or will his name be Jonah
Crying to repent
On the Island of Iona?

Will his name be Jason
Looking for a seaman
Or a mad crusader
Without rhyme or reason?

What will be his message –
War or work or marriage?
News as new as dawn
Or an old adage?

Will he give a champion
Answer to my question
Or will his words be dark
And his ways evasion?

Will his name be Love
And all his talk be crazy?
Or will his name be Death
And his message easy?

LOUIS MACNEICE

Little Fan

'I don't like the look of little Fan, mother,
   I don't like her looks a little bit.
Her face – well, it's not exactly different,
   But there's something wrong with it.

'She went down to the sea-shore yesterday,
   And she talked to somebody there,
Now she won't do anything but sit
   And comb out her yellowy hair.

'Her eyes are shiny and she sings, mother,
   Like nobody ever sang before.
Perhaps they gave her something queer to eat,
   Down by the rocks on the shore.

'Speak to me, speak, little Fan dear,
   Aren't you feeling very well?
Where have you been and what are you singing,
   And what's that seaweedy smell?

'Where did you get that shiny comb, love,
  And those pretty coral beads so red?
Yesterday you had two legs, I'm certain,
  But now there's something else instead.

'I don't like the looks of little Fan, mother,
  You'd best go and close the door.
Watch now, or she'll be gone for ever
  To the rocks by the brown sandy shore.'

JAMES REEVES

Kinder- und Hausmärchen
(Grimm's Fairy Tales)

Night gathers. Outside
All is comfortless:
Rain-dark, and the wide
Flat fields of weariness.

But here – at the fire –
Tom Cat, Curly-locks,
Old Aunt Maria
Wait for the story-box.

Then out come leaping
In raiment of words
Frog-princes, sleeping
Princesses, weeping
Sisters, and creeping
Witches, and cheeping,
Cackling, crying,
Singing, sighing,
Triumphantly flying
Magical birds.

BRIAN ALDERSON

Her-zie

A troll and his wife speak of the human child they stole.

What's wrong with you-zie?
Nothing with me-zie,
Then what with who-zie?
Only with Her-zie,
So what with Her-zie?
A hearse for her-zie
A hearse for her-zie
Came for her.

What colour was it then?
Golden, golden,
Was there anyone in it?
A pale king was in it.
That was not a hearse for Her-zie, husband,
It was her marriage carriage.
It was a hearse for me, then,
My heart went with them and died then.

Husband, ah me-zie,
Your heart has died for Her-zie,
Without it you cannot be easy.

STEVIE SMITH

[167]

Counsel

The face in the water said
(rather fretfully, I thought):
'Be courteous to crone and spider,
Prudent with keys,
Free the hooked fish and such –
Of course you know all about that;

And *do* be careful when wishing.
In spite of all the examples
They *never* learn.
It takes imagination
To start with the fourth guess, thought of later,
The fourth wish, after the moral.

NAOMI LEWIS

Desire

The knight knocked at the castle gate;
The lady marvelled who was thereat.

To call the porter he would not blin[1];
The lady said he should not come in.

The portress was a lady bright;
Strangeness that lady hight.

She asked him what was his name;
He said 'Desire, your man, Madame.'

She said 'Desire, what do ye here?'
He said 'Madame, as your prisoner.'

He was counselled to brief a bill,
And show my lady his own will.

'Kindness,' said she, 'would it bear,'
'And Pity,' said she, 'would be there.'

Thus how they did we cannot say;
We left them there and went our way.

WILLIAM CORNISH

[1]cease

[169]

From Prothalamion

Calm was the day, and through the trembling air
Sweet breathing Zephyrus did softly play,
A gentle spirit, that lightly did delay
Hot Titan's beams, which then did glister fair;
When I whose sullen care,
Through discontent of my long fruitless stay
In prince's court, and expectation vain
Of idle hopes, which still do fly away
Like empty shadows, did afflict my brain,
Walked forth to ease my pain
Along the shore of silver streaming Thames,
Whose rutty bank, the which his river hems,
Was painted all with variable flowers,
And all the meads adorned with dainty gems,
Fit to deck maidens' bowers,
And crown their paramours,
Against the bridal day, which is not long:
   Sweet Thames, run softly, till I end my song.

There, in a meadow, by the river's side,
A flock of nymphs I chanced to espy,
All lovely daughters of the flood thereby,
With goodly greenish locks all loose untied,
As each had been a bride;
And each one had a little wicker basket,
Made of fine twigs entrailed curiously,
In which they gathered flowers to fill their flasket,
And with fine fingers cropped full featously
The tender stalks on high.
Of every sort, which in that meadow grew,
They gathered some; the violet pallid blue,
The little daisy, that at evening closes,

The virgin lily, and the primrose true,
With store of vermeil roses,
To deck their bridegrooms' posies,
Against the bridal day, which was not long:
 Sweet Thames, run softly, till I end my song.

With that, I saw two swans of goodly hue
Come softly swimming down along the Lee;
Two fairer birds I yet did never see.
The snow, which doth the top of Pindus strew,
Did never whiter shew,
Nor Jove himself, when he a swan would be
For love of Leda, whiter did appear:
Yet Leda was they say as white as he,
Yet not so white as these, nor nothing near.
So purely white they were,
That even the gentle stream, the which them bare,
Seemed foul to them, and bade his billows spare
To wet their silken feathers, lest they might
Soil their fair plumes with water not so fair,
And mar their beauties bright,
That shone as heaven's light,
Against their bridal day, which was not long:
 Sweet Thames, run softly, till I end my song. . . .

Then forth they all out of their baskets drew
Great store of flowers, the honour of the field,
That to the sense did fragrant odours yield,
All which upon those goodly birds they threw,
And all the waves did strew,
That like old Peneus' waters they did seem,
When down along by pleasant Tempe's shore,
Scattered with flowers, through Thessaly they stream,
That they appear through lilies' plenteous store,
Like a bride's chamber floor.

Two of those nymphs, meanwhile, two garlands bound,
Of freshest flowers which in that mead they found,
The which presenting all in trim array,
Their snowy foreheads therewithal they crowned,
Whilst one did sing this lay,
Prepared against that day,
Against their bridal day, which was not long:
  Sweet Thames, run softly, till I end my song. . . .

At length they all to merry London came,
To merry London, my most kindly nurse,
That to me gave this life's first native source;
Though from another place I take my name,
An house of ancient fame.
There when they came, whereas those bricky towers,
The which on Thames' broad aged back do ride,
Where now the studious lawyers have their bowers
There whilom wont the Templar Knights to bide,
Till they decayed through pride:
Next whereunto there stands a stately place,
Where oft I gained gifts and goodly grace
Of that great lord, which therein wont to dwell,
Whose want too well now feels my friendless case.
But ah! here fits not well
Old woes but joys to tell
Against the bridal day, which is not long:
  Sweet Thames, run softly, till I end my song.

Yet therein now doth lodge a noble peer,
Great England's glory and the world's wide wonder,
Whose dreadful name late through all Spain did thunder,
And Hercules' two pillars standing near
Did make to quake and fear.
Fair branch of honour, flower of chivalry,
That fillest England with thy triumph's fame,

[172]

Joy have thou of thy noble victory,
And endless happiness of thine own name
That promiseth the same:
That through thy prowess and victorious arms,
Thy country may be freed from foreign harms;
And great Elisa's glorious name may ring
Through all the world, filled with thy wide alarms,
Which some brave Muse may sing
To ages following,
Upon the bridal day, which is not long:
   Sweet Thames, run softly, till I end my song.

From those high towers this noble lord issuing,
Like radiant Hesper when his golden hair
In th' Ocean billows he hath bathed fair,
Descended to the river's open viewing,
With a great train ensuing.
Above the rest were goodly to be seen
Two gentle knights of lovely face and feature
Beseeming well the bower of any queen,
With gifts of wit and ornaments of nature,
Fit for so goodly stature;
That like the twins of Jove they seemed in sight,
Which deck the baldric of the heavens bright.
They two forth pacing to the river's side,
Received those two fair birds, their love's delight,
Which at th'appointed tide
Each one did make his bride,
Against their bridal day, which is not long:
   Sweet Thames, run softly, till I end my song.

EDMUND SPENSER

Farewell

What should I say,
 Since faith is dead,
And truth away
 From you is fled:
 Should I be led
  With doubleness?
  Nay, nay, mistress!

I promised you,
 And you promised me,
To be as true,
 As I would be.
 But since I see
  Your double heart,
  Farewell my part!

Thought for to take
 It is not my mind,
But to forsake
 One so unkind,
 And as I find
  So will I trust,
  Farewell, unjust!

Can ye say nay,
 But that you said
That I alway
 Should be obeyed?
 And thus betrayed,
  Or that I wist,
  Farewell, unkissed!

SIR THOMAS WYATT

As I Walked Out One Night

As I walked out one night, it being dark all over,
The moon did show no light I could discover,
Down by a river-side where ships were sailing,
A lonely maid I spied, weeping and bewailing.

I boldly stept up to her, and asked what grieved her,
She made this reply, None could relieve her,
'For my love is pressed,' she cried, 'to cross the ocean,
My mind is like the Sea, always in motion.'

He said, 'My pretty fair maid, mark well my story,
For your true love and I fought for England's glory,
By one unlucky shot we both got parted,
And by the wounds he got, I'm broken hearted.

'He told me before he died, his heart was broken,
He gave me this gold ring, take it for a token, –
"Take this unto my dear, there is no one fairer,
Tell her to be kind and love the bearer."'

Soon as these words he spoke she ran distracted,
Not knowing what she did, nor how she acted,
She run ashore, her hair showing her anger,
'Young man, you've come too late, for I'll wed no stranger.'

Soon as these words she spoke, his love grew stronger,
He flew into her arms, he could wait no longer,
They both sat down and sung, but she sung clearest,
Like a nightingale in spring, 'Welcome home, my dearest.'

He sang, 'God bless the wind that blew him over.'
She sang, 'God bless the ship that brought him over.'
They both sat down and sung but she sung clearest,
Like a nightingale in spring, 'Welcome home, my dearest.'

ANON

From The Statue and the Bust

There's a palace in Florence, the world knows well,
And a statue watches it from the square,
And this story of both do our townsmen tell.

Ages ago, a lady there,
At the farthest window facing the East
Asked, 'Who rides by with the royal air?'

The brides-maids' prattle around her ceased;
She leaned forth, one on either hand;
They saw how the blush of the bride increased –

They felt by its beats her heart expand –
As one at each ear and both in a breath
Whispered, 'The Great-Duke Ferdinand.'

That selfsame instant, underneath,
The Duke rode past in his idle way,
Empty and fine like a swordless sheath.

Gay he rode, with a friend as gay,
Till he threw his head back – 'Who is she?'
– 'A Bride the Riccardi brings home to-day.'

Hair in heaps lay heavily
Over a pale brow spirit-pure –
Carved like the heart of the coal-black tree,

Crisped like a war-steed's encolure –
And vainly sought to dissemble her eyes
Of the blackest black our eyes endure.

And lo, a blade for a knight's emprise
Filled the fine empty sheath of a man, –
The Duke grew straightway brave and wise.

He looked at her, as a lover can;
She looked at him, as one who awakes, –
The Past was a sleep, and her life began.

Now, love so ordered for both their sakes,
A feast was held that selfsame night
In the pile which the mighty shadow makes. . . .

The Duke (with the statue's face in the square)
Turned in the midst of his multitude
At the bright approach of the bridal pair.

Face to face the lovers stood
A single minute and no more,
While the bridegroom bent as a man subdued –

Bowed till his bonnet brushed the floor –
For the Duke on the lady a kiss conferred,
As the courtly custom was of yore.

In a minute can lovers exchange a word?
If a word did pass, which I do not think,
Only one out of the thousand heard.

That was the bridegroom. At day's brink
He and his bride were alone at last
In a bed-chamber by a taper's blink.

Calmly he said that her lot was cast,
That the door she had passed was shut on her
Till the final catafalk repassed.

The world meanwhile, its noise and stir,
Through a certain window facing the East
She could watch like a convent's chronicler.

Since passing the door might lead to a feast,
And a feast might lead to so much beside,
He, of many evils, chose the least.

'Freely I choose too,' said the bride –
'Your window and its world suffice,'
Replied the tongue, while the heart replied –

'If I spend the night with that devil twice,
May his window serve as my loop of hell
Whence a damned soul looks on Paradise!

'I fly to the Duke who loves me well,
Sit by his side and laugh at sorrow
Ere I count another ave-bell.

''Tis only the coat of a page to borrow,
And tie my hair in a horse-boy's trim,
And I save my soul – but not tomorrow' –

(She checked herself and her eye grew dim) –
'My father tarries to bless my state:
I must keep it one day more for him.

'Is one day more so long to wait?
Moreover the Duke rides past, I know;
We shall see each other, sure as fate.'

She turned on her side and slept. Just so!
So we resolve on a thing and sleep:
So did the lady, ages ago.

That night the Duke said, 'Dear or cheap
As the cost of this cup of bliss may prove
To body or soul, I will drain it deep.'

And on the morrow, bold with love,
He beckoned the bridegroom (close on call,
As his duty bade, by the Duke's alcove)

And smiled 'Twas a very funeral,
Your lady will think, this feast of ours, –
A shame to efface, what'er befall!

'What if we break from the Arno bowers,
And try if Petraja, cool and green,
Cure last night's fault with this morning's flowers?'

The bridegroom, not a thought to be seen
On his steady brow and quiet mouth,
Said, 'Too much favour for me so mean!

'But, alas! my lady leaves the South;
Each wind that comes from the Apennine
Is a menace to her tender youth. . . .

Quoth the Duke, 'A sage and a kindly fear.
Moreover Petraja is cold this spring;
Be our feast to-night as usual here!'

And then to himself – 'Which night shall bring
Thy bride to her lover's embraces, fool –
Or I am the fool, and thou art the king!

'Yet my passion must wait a night, nor cool –
For to-night the Envoy arrives from France,
Whose heart I unlock with thyself, my tool.

'I need thee still and might miss per chance.
To-day is not wholly lost, beside,
With its hope of my lady's countenance. . . .'

Be sure that each renewed the vow,
No morrow's sun should arise and set
And leave them then as it left them now.

But next day passed, and next day yet,
With still fresh cause to wait one day more
Ere each leaped over the parapet.

And still, as love's brief morning wore,
With a gentle start, half smile, half sigh,
They found love not as it seemed before.

They thought it would work infallibly,
But not in despite of heaven and earth –
The rose would blow when the storm passed by.

Meantime they could profit in winter's dearth
By winter's fruits that supplant the rose:
The world and its ways have a certain worth! . . .

Meantime, worse fates than a lover's fate,
Who daily may ride and pass and look
Where his lady watches behind the grate!

And she – she watched the square like a book
Holding one picture and only one,
Which daily to find she undertook. . . .

So weeks grew months, years – gleam by gleam
The glory dropped from their youth and love,
And both perceived they had dreamed a dream. . . .

One day as the lady saw her youth
Depart, and the silver thread that streaked
Her hair, and, worn by the serpent's tooth,

The brow so puckered, the chin so peaked, –
And wondered who the woman was,
Hollow-eyed and haggard-cheeked,

Fronting her silent in the glass –
'Summon here,' she suddenly said,
'Before the rest of my old self pass,

'Him, the Carver, a hand to aid,
Who fashions the clay no love will change,
And fixes a beauty never to fade.

'Let Robbia's craft so apt and strange
Arrest the remains of young and fair,
And rivet them while the seasons range.

'Make me a face on the window there,
Waiting as ever, mute the while,
My love to pass below in the square! . . .

'Where is the use of the lip's red charm,
The heaven of hair, the pride of the brow,
And the blood that blues the inside arm –

'Unless we turn, as the soul knows how,
The earthly gift to an end divine?
A lady of clay is as good, I trow.'

But long ere Robbia's cornice, fine
With flowers and fruits which leaves enlace,
Was set where now is the empty shrine –

And, leaning out of a bright blue space,
As a ghost might lean from a chink of sky,
The passionate pale lady's face –

Eyeing ever with earnest eye
And quick-turned neck at its breathless stretch,
Some one who ever is passing by –

The Duke had sighed like the simplest wretch
In Florence, 'Youth – my dream escapes!
Will its record stay?' And he bade them fetch

Some subtle moulder of brazen shapes –
'Can the soul, the will, die out of a man
Ere his body find the grave that gapes?

'John of Douay shall effect my plan,
Set me on horseback here aloft,
Alive, as the crafty sculptor can,

'In the very square I have crossed so oft!
That men may admire, when future suns
Shall touch the eyes to a purpose soft,

[181]

'While the mouth and the brow stay brave in bronze –
Admire and say, "When he was alive,
How he would take his pleasure once!"

'And it shall go hard but I contrive
To listen the while and laugh in my tomb
At idleness which aspires to strive.'

So! while these wait the trump of doom,
How do their spirits pass, I wonder,
Nights and days in the narrow room?

Still, I suppose, they sit and ponder
What a gift life was, ages ago,
Six steps out of the chapel yonder.

Only they see not God, I know,
Nor all that chivalry of His,
The soldier-saints who, row on row,

Burn upward each to his point of bliss –
Since, the end of life being manifest,
He had burned his way thro' the world to this.

I hear you reproach, 'But delay was best,
For their end was a crime.' – Oh, a crime will do
As well, I reply, to serve for a test,

As a virtue golden through and through,
Sufficient to vindicate itself
And prove its worth at a moment's view! ...

Stake your counter as boldly every whit,
Venture as truly, use the same skill,
Do your best, whether winning or losing it,

If you choose to play! – is my principle.
Let a man contend to the uttermost
For his life's set prize, be it what it will!

The counter our lovers staked was lost
As surely as if it were lawful coin:
And the sin I impute to each frustrate ghost

Is, the unlit lamp and the ungirt loin,
Though the end in sight was a vice, I say.
You of the virtue, (we issue join)
How strive you? *De te, fabula!*[1]

ROBERT BROWNING

[1]This story concerns you.

Lost Love

His eyes are quickened so with grief,
He can watch a grass or leaf
Every instant grow; he can
Clearly through a flint wall see,
Or watch the startled spirit flee
From the throat of a dead man.

Across two counties he can hear
And catch your words before you speak.
The woodlouse or the maggot's weak
Clamour rings in his sad ear,
And noise so slight it would surpass
Credence – drinking sound of grass,
Worm talk, clashing jaws of moth
Chumbling holes in cloth;
The groan of ants who undertake
Gigantic loads for honour's sake,
(Their sinews creak, their breath comes thin);

[183]

Whir of spiders when they spin,
And minute whispering, mumbling, sighs
Of idle grubs and flies.

This man is quickened so with grief,
He wanders god-like or like thief
Inside and out, below, above,
Without relief seeking lost love.

ROBERT GRAVES

We Saw the Swallows Gathering in the Sky

We saw the swallows gathering in the sky,
And in the osier-isle we heard them noise.
We had not to look back on summer joys,
Or forward to a summer of bright dye:
But in the largeness of the evening earth
Our spirits grew as we went side by side.
The hour became her husband and my bride.
Love, that had robbed us so, thus blessed our dearth!
The pilgrims of the year waxed very loud
In multitudinous chatterings, as the flood
Full brown came from the West, and like pale blood
Expanded to the upper crimson cloud.
Love, that had robbed us of immortal things,
This little moment mercifully gave,
Where I have seen across the twilight wave
The swan sail with her young beneath her wings. . . .

Thus piteously Love closed what he begat:
The union of this ever-diverse pair!
These two were rapid falcons in a snare,
Condemned to do the flitting of the bat.
Lovers beneath the singing sky of May,
They wandered once; clear as the dew on flowers;
But they fed not on the advancing hours:
Their hearts held cravings for the buried day.
Then each applied to each that fatal knife,
Deep questioning, which probes to endless dole.
Ah, what a dusty answer gets the soul
When hot for certainties in this our life! –
In tragic hints here see what evermore
Moves dark as yonder midnight ocean's force,
Thundering like ramping hosts of warrior horse,
To throw that faint thin line upon the shore!

from *Modern Love*

Meeting

If we shall live, we live:
   If we shall die, we die:
If we live we shall meet again:
   But to-night, good-bye.
One word, let but one be heard –
   What, not one word?

If we sleep we shall wake again
    And see to-morrow's light:
If we wake, we shall meet again:
    But to-night, good-night.
    Good-night, my lost and found –
      Still not a sound?

If we live, we must part:
If we die, we part in pain:
    If we die, we shall part
    Only to meet again.
By those tears on either cheek,
    To-morrow you will speak.

To meet, worth living for:
   Worth dying for, to meet.
To meet, worth parting for:
Bitter forgot in sweet.
To meet, worth parting before,
Never to part more.

CHRISTINA ROSSETTI

Chinese Ballad

Now he has seen the girl Hsiang-Hsiang:
Now back to the guerrilla band.
And she goes with him down the vale.
And pauses at the strand.

The mud is yellow, broad, and thick,
And their feet stick, where the stream turns.
'Make me two models out of this,
That clutches as it yearns.

'Make one of me and one of you,
And both shall be alive
Were there no magic in the dolls
The children would not thrive.

'When you make them smash them back;
They yet can live again.
Again make dolls of you and me,
But mix them grain by grain.

'So your flesh will be part of mine,
And part of mine be yours.
Brother and sister we shall be,
Whose unity endures.

'Always the sister doll will cry,
Made in these careful ways,
Cry on and on, come back to me,
Come back, in a few days.'

MAO TSE TUNG
translated by William Empson

Plucking the Rushes
A boy and girl are sent to gather rushes for thatching

Green rushes with red shoots,
Long leaves bending to the wind –
You and I in the same boat
Plucking rushes at the Five Lakes.
We started at dawn from the orchid-island:

We rested under the elms till noon.
You and I plucking rushes
Had not plucked a handful when night came!

ANON
translated by Arthur Waley

A Serenade at the Villa

That was I, you heard last night
  When there rose no moon at all
Nor, to pierce the strained and tight
  Tent of heaven, a planet small:
Life was dead, and so was light.

Not a twinkle from the fly,
  Not a glimmer from the worm.
When the crickets stopped their cry,
  When the owls forbore a term,
You heard music; that was I.

Earth turned in her sleep with pain,
  Sultrily suspired for proof:
In at heaven and out again,
  Lightning! – where it broke the roof,
Bloodlike, some few drops of rain.

What they could my words expressed,
  O my Love, my All, my One!
Singing helped the verses best,
  And when singing's best was done,
To my lute I left the rest.

So wore night; the East was gray,
    White the broad-faced hemlock flowers;
There would be another day;
    Ere its first of heavy hours
Found me, I had past away.

What became of all the hopes,
    Words and song and lute as well?
Say, this struck you – 'When life gropes
    Feebly for the path where fell
Light last on the evening slopes,

'One friend in that path shall be
    To secure my steps from wrong;
One to count night day for me,
    Patient through the watches long,
Serving most with none to see.'

Never say – as something bodes –
    'So, the worst has yet a worse!
When life halts 'neath double loads,
    Better the task-master's curse
Than such music on the roads!

'When no moon succeeds the sun,
    Nor can pierce the midnight's tent
Any star, the smallest one,
    While some drops, where lightning went,
Show the final storm begun –

'When the fire-fly hides its spot,
    When the garden-voices fail
In the darkness thick and hot, –
    Shall another voice avail,
That shape be where these are not?

'Has some plague a longer lease
    Proffering its help uncouth?
Can't one even die in peace?
    As one shuts one's eyes on youth,
Is that face the last one sees?'

Oh, how dark your villa was,
    Windows fast and obdurate!
How the garden grudged me grass
    Where I stood – the iron gate
Ground its teeth to let me pass!

ROBERT BROWNING

The Conformers

Yes; we'll wed, my little fay,
    And you shall write you mine,
And in a villa chastely gray
    We'll house, and sleep, and dine.
    But those night-screened, divine,
Stolen trysts of heretofore,
We of choice ecstasies and fine
        Shall know no more.

The formal faced cohue
    Will then no more upbraid
With smiting smiles and whisperings two
    Who have thrown less loves in shade.
    We shall no more evade
    The searching light of the sun,
Our game of passion will be played,
        Our dreaming done.

[190]

We shall not go in stealth
    To rendezvous unknown,
But friends will ask me of your health,
    And you about my own.
    When we abide alone,
    No leapings each to each,
But syllables in frigid tone
        Of household speech.

When down to dust we glide
    Men will not say askance,
As now: 'How all the country side
    Rings with their mad romance!'
    But as they graveward glance
    Remark: 'In them we lose
A worthy pair, who helped advance
        Sound parish views.'

THOMAS HARDY

It is the Evening Hour

It is the evening hour,
    How silent all doth lie:
The hornèd moon she shows her face
    In the river with the sky.
Just by the path on which we pass,
The flaggy lake lies still as glass.

Spirit of her I love,
    Whispering to me
Stories of sweet visions as I rove,

Here stop, and crop with me
Sweet flowers that in the still hour grew –
We'll take them home, nor shake off the bright dew.

Mary, or sweet spirit of thee,
    As the bright sun shines to-morrow
Thy dark eyes these flowers shall see,
    Gathered by me in sorrow,
In the still hour when my mind was free
To walk alone – yet wish I walked with thee.

JOHN CLARE

The Combat

It was not meant for human eyes,
That combat on the shabby patch
Of clods and trampled turf that lies
Somewhere beneath the sodden skies
For eye of toad or adder to catch.

And having seen it I accuse
The crested animal in his pride,
Arrayed in all the royal hues
Which hide the claws he well can use
To tear the heart out of the side.

Body of leopard, eagle's head
And whetted beak, and lion's mane,
And frost-grey hedge of feathers spread
Behind – he seemed of all things bred.
I shall not see his like again.

As for his enemy, there came in
A soft round beast as brown as clay;
All rent and patched his wretched skin;
A battered bag he might have been,
Some old used thing to throw away.

[193]

Yet he awaited face to face
The furious beast and the swift attack.
Soon over and done. That was no place
Or time for chivalry or for grace.
The fury had him on his back.

And two small paws like hands flew out
To right and left as the trees stood by.
One would have said beyond a doubt
This was the very end of the bout,
But that the creature would not die.

For ere the death-stroke he was gone,
Writhed, whirled, huddled into his den,
Safe somehow there. The fight was done,
And he had lost who had all but won.
But oh his deadly fury then.

A while the place lay blank, forlorn,
Drowsing as in relief from pain.
The cricket chirped, the grating thorn
Stirred, and a little sound was born.
The champions took their posts again.

And all began. The stealthy paw
Slashed out and in. Could nothing save
These rags and tatters from the claw?
Nothing. And yet I never saw
A beast so helpless and so brave.

And now, while the trees stand watching, still
The unequal battle rages there.
The killing beast that cannot kill
Swells and swells in his fury till
You'd almost think it was despair.

EDWIN MUIR

Noah

They gathered around and told him not to do it,
They formed a committee and tried to take control,
They cancelled his building permit and they stole
His plans, I sometimes wonder he got through it.
He told them wrath was coming, they would rue it,
He begged them to believe the tides would roll,
He offered them passage to his destined goal,
A new world. They were finished and he knew it.
All to no end.   And then the rain began.
A spatter at first that barely wet the soil,
Then showers, quick rivulets lacing the town,
Then deluge universal. The old man
Arthritic from his years of scorn and toil
Leaned from the admiral's walk and watched them drown.

ROY DANIELLS

From The Masque of Anarchy
Written on the occasion of the massacre at Manchester

As I lay asleep in Italy
There came a voice from over the Sea,
And with great power it forth led me
To walk in the visions of Poesy.

I met Murder on the way –
He had a mask like Castlereagh –
Very smooth he looked, yet grim;
Seven blood-hounds followed him:

All were fat; and well they might
Be in admirable plight,
For one by one, and two by two,
He tossed them human hearts to chew
Which from his wide cloak he drew.

Next came Fraud, and he had on,
Like Eldon, an ermined gown;
His big tears, for he wept well,
Turned to mill-stones as they fell.

And the little children, who
Round his feet played to and fro,
Thinking every tear a gem,
Had their brains knocked out by them. . . .

Last came Anarchy: he rode
On a white horse, splashed with blood;
He was pale even to the lips,
Like Death in the Apocalypse.

And he wore a kingly crown;
And in his grasp a sceptre shone;
On his brow this mark I saw –
'I AM GOD, AND KING, AND LAW!'

And a mighty troop around,
With their trampling shook the ground,
Waving each a bloody sword,
For the service of their Lord. . . .

And Anarchy, the Skeleton,
Bowed and grinned to every one,
As well as if his education
Had cost ten millions to the nation. . . .

PERCY BYSSHE SHELLY

This was written in response to the 'Battle of Peterloo'
in 1819. A crowd in St Peter's Fields outside Man-
chester was attacked by the Yeomanry on the orders of
the local magistrates; eleven people were killed.
Castlereagh and Eldon were leading ministers in the
government of the day, which congratulated the
magistrates on their action.

London

I wander thro' each charter'd street,
Near where the charter'd Thames does flow,
And mark in every face I meet
Marks of weakness, marks of woe.

In every cry of every Man,
In every Infant's cry of fear,
In every voice, in every ban,
The mind-forg'd manacles I hear.

How the Chimney-sweeper's cry
Every black'ning Church appalls;
And the hapless Soldier's sigh
Runs in blood down Palace walls.

But most thro' midnight streets I hear
How the youthful Harlot's curse
Blasts the new born Infant's tear,
And blights with plagues the Marriage hearse.

WILLIAM BLAKE

From The Rubáiyát of Omar Khayyam

Awake! for Morning in the Bowl of Night
Has flung the Stone that puts the Stars to Flight:
   And Lo! the Hunter of the East has caught
The Sultán's Turret in a Noose of Light. . . .

Come, fill the Cup, and in the Fire of Spring
The Winter Garment of Repentance fling:
   The Bird of Time has but a little way
To fly – and Lo! the Bird is on the Wing.

And look – a thousand Blossoms with the Day
Woke – and a thousand scatter'd into Clay:
   And this first Summer Month that Brings the Rose
Shall take Jamshýd and Kaikobád away. . . .

'How sweet is mortal Sovranty!' – think some:
Others – 'How blest the Paradise to come!'
   Ah, take the Cash in hand and waive the Rest;
Oh, the brave Music of a *distant* Drum! . . .

The Worldly Hope men set their Hearts upon
Turns Ashes – or it prospers; and anon,
   Like Snow upon the Desert's dusty Face
Lighting a little Hour or two – is gone. . . .

Think, in this batter'd Caravanserai
Whose Doorways are alternate Night and Day,
   How Sultán after Sultán with his Pomp
Abode his Hour or two, and went his way.

They say the Lion and the Lizard keep
The Courts where Jamshýd gloried and drank deep;
   And Bahrám, that great Hunter – the Wild Ass
Stamps o'er his Head, and he lies fast asleep.

I sometimes think that never blows so red
The Rose as where some buried Cæsar bled;
   That every Hyacinth the Garden wears
Dropt in its Lap from some once lovely Head. . . .

Alike for those who for TO-DAY prepare,
And those that after a TO-MORROW stare,
   A Muezzin from the Tower of Darkness cries
'Fools! your Reward is neither Here nor There!' . . .

Oh, come with old Khayyám, and leave the Wise
To talk; one thing is certain, that Life flies;
   One thing is certain, and the Rest is Lies;
The Flower that once has blown for ever dies.

Myself when young did eagerly frequent
Doctor and Saint, and heard great Argument
   About it and about: but evermore
Came out by the same Door as in I went.

With them the Seed of Wisdom did I sow,
And with my own hand labour'd it to grow:
   And this was all the Harvest that I reap'd –
'I came like Water, and like Wind I go.'

Into this Universe, and *why* not knowing,
Nor *whence*, like Water willy-nilly flowing:
   And out of it, as Wind along the Waste,
I know not *whither*, willy-nilly blowing.

What, without asking, hither hurried *whence*?
And, without asking, *whither* hurried hence?
   Another and another Cup to drown
The Memory of this Impertinence!

Up from Earth's Centre through the Seventh Gate
I rose, and on the Throne of Saturn sate,
    And many Knots unravel'd by the Road;
But not the Knot of Human Death and Fate.

There was a Door to which I found no Key:
There was a Veil past which I could not see:
    Some little Talk awhile of ME and THEE
There seem'd – and then no more of THEE and ME. . . .

One Moment in Annihilation's Waste,
One Moment, of the Well of Life to taste –
    The Stars are setting and the Caravan
Starts for the Dawn of Nothing – Oh, make haste! . . .

'Tis all a Chequer-board of Nights and Days
Where Destiny with Men for Pieces plays:
    Higher and thither moves, and mates and slays,
And one by one back in the Closet lays.

The Ball no Question makes of Ayes and Noes,
But Right or Left as strikes the Player goes;
    And He that toss'd Thee down into the Field,
He knows about it all – HE knows – HE knows!

The Moving Finger writes; and, having writ,
Moves on: nor all thy Piety nor Wit
    Shall lure it back to cancel half a Line,
Nor all thy Tears wash out a Word of it.

And that inverted Bowl we call The Sky,
Whereunder crawling coop't we live and die,
    Lift not thy hands to *It* for help – for It
Rolls impotently on as Thou or I. . . .

Listen again. One evening at the Close
Of Ramazán, ere the better Moon arose,
　　In that old Potter's Shop I stood alone
With the clay Population round in Rows.

And, strange to tell, among that Earthen Lot
Some could articulate, while others not:
　　And suddenly one more impatient cried –
'Who *is* the Potter, pray, and who the Pot?'

Then said another – 'Surely not in vain
My Substance from the common Earth was ta'en,
　　That He who subtly wrought me into Shape
Should stamp me back to common Earth again.'

Another said – 'Why, ne'er a peevish Boy,
Would break the Bowl from which he drank in Joy;
　　Shall He that *made* the Vessel in pure Love
And Fancy, in an after Rage destroy!'

None answer'd this; but after Silence spake
A Vessel of a more ungainly Make:
　　'They sneer at me for leaning all awry;
What! did the Hand then of the Potter shake?' . . .

Ah, with the Grape my fading Life provide,
And wash my Body whence the Life has died,
　　And in a Winding-sheet of Vine-leaf wrapt,
So bury me by some sweet Garden-side. . . .

And much as Wine has play'd the Infidel,
And Robb'd me of my Robe of Honour – well,
　　I often wonder what the Vintners buy
One half so precious as the Goods they sell.

Alas, that Spring should vanish with the Rose!
That Youth's sweet-scented Manuscript should close!
  The Nightingale that in the Branches sang,
Ah, whence, and whither flown again, who knows! . . .

Ah, Moon of my Delight, who know'st no wane,
The Moon of Heav'n is rising once again:
  How oft hereafter rising shall she look
Through this same Garden after me – in vain!

And when Thyself with shining Foot shall pass
Among the Guests Star-scatter'd on the Grass,
  And in thy joyous Errand reach the Spot
Where I made one – turn down an empty Glass!

EDWARD FITZGERALD

Song

Rarely, rarely, comest thou,
  Spirit of Delight!
Wherefore hast thou left me now
  Many a day and night?
Many a weary night and day
'Tis since thou art fled away.

How shall ever one like me
  Win thee back again?
With the joyous and the free
  Thou wilt scoff at pain.
Spirit false! thou hast forgot
All but those who need thee not.

As a lizard with the shade
   Of a trembling leaf,
Thou with sorrow art dismayed;
   Even the sighs of grief
Reproach thee, that thou art not near,
And reproach thou wilt not hear.

Let me set my mournful ditty
   To a merry measure,
Thou wilt never come for pity,
   Thou wilt come for pleasure.
Pity then will cut away
Those cruel wings, and thou wilt stay.

I love all that thou lovest,
   Spirit of Delight!
The fresh Earth in new leaves drest,
   And the starry night;
Autumn evening, and the morn
When the golden mists are born.

I love snow, and all the forms
   Of the radiant frost;
I love waves, and winds, and storms.
   Every thing almost
Which is Nature's, and may be
Untainted by man's misery.

I love tranquil solitude,
   And such society
As is quiet, wise and good.
   Between thee and me
What difference? but thou dost possess
The things I seek, not love them less.

I love Love – though he has wings,
    And like light can flee,
But above all other things,
    Spirit, I love thee –
Thou art love and life! O come
Make once more my heart thy home.

PERCY BYSSHE SHELLEY

The Pulley

When God at first made man,
Having a glass of blessings standing by,
'Let us,' said he, 'pour on him all we can;
Let the world's riches, which dispersèd lie,
    Contract into a span.'

So strength first made a way,
Then beauty flowed, then wisdom, honour, pleasure;
When almost all was out, God made a stay,
Perceiving that, alone of all his treasure,
    Rest in the bottom lay.

'For if I should,' said he,
'Bestow this jewel also on my creature,
He would adore my gifts instead of me,
And rest in Nature, not the God of Nature;
    So both should losers be.

'Yet let him keep the rest,
But keep them with repining, restlessness;
Let him be rich and weary, that at least,
If goodness lead him not, yet weariness
    May toss him to my breast.'

GEORGE HERBERT

[205]

The Sluggard

'Tis the voice of the Sluggard; I heard him complain,
'You have waked me too soon; I must slumber again;'
As the Door on its Hinges, so he on his Bed,
Turns his Sides, and his Shoulders, and his heavy Head.

'A little more Sleep, and a little more Slumber';
Thus he wastes half his Days, and his Hours without
    Number;
And when he gets up, he sits folding his Hands,
Or walks about saunt'ring, or trifling he stands.

I passed by his Garden, and saw the wild Briar
The Thorn and the Thistle grow broader and higher;
The Clothes that hang on him are turning to Rags;
And his Money still wastes, till he starves or he begs.

I made him a Visit, still hoping to find
That he took better Care for improving his Mind;
He told me his Dreams, talked of Eating and Drinking;
But he scarce reads his Bible, and never loves Thinking.

Said I then to my Heart, 'Here's a Lesson for me;
That Man's but a Picture of what I might be;
But thanks to my Friends for their Care in my Breeding,
Who taught me betimes to love Working and Reading.'

ISAAC WATTS

Most of the strange songs and ballads in Lewis Carroll's 'Alice' books
are parodied versions of pious, moral, 'improving' rhymes, well
known to every well-brought-up child of the early nineteenth century.
Carroll, a clergyman's son and a clergyman himself, clearly enjoyed
this daring private joke, and sharing it with the young. In some cases,
though – and this is one – the original is today rather more interesting
than the parody. *'Tis the voice of the lobster* has long lost the edge of its
humour; but the sluggard of Watts's poem, drop-out and dreamer,
seems an ominously modern portrait.

Humpty Dumpty's Poem

In winter, when the fields are white,
I sing this song for your delight –

* * *

In spring, when woods are getting green,
I'll try and tell you what I mean.

* * *

In summer, when the days are long,
Perhaps you'll understand the song:

In autumn, when the leaves are brown,
Take pen and ink, and write it down.

* * *

I sent a message to the fish:
I told them 'This is what I wish.'

The little fishes of the sea,
They sent an answer back to me.

The little fishes' answer was
'We cannot do it, Sir, because –'

* * *

I sent to them again to say
'It will be better to obey.'

The fishes answered with a grin,
'Why, what a temper you are in!'

I told them once, I told them twice:
They would not listen to advice.

I took a kettle large and new,
Fit for the deed I had to do.

My heart went hop, my heart went thump:
I filled the kettle at the pump.

Then someone came to me and said,
'The little fishes are in bed.'

I said to him, I said it plain,
'Then you must wake them up again.'

I said it very loud and clear;
I went and shouted in his ear.

       *   *   *

But he was very stiff and proud;
He said 'You needn't shout so loud!'

And he was very proud and stiff;
He said 'I'd go and wake them, if –'

I took a corkscrew from the shelf;
I went to wake them up myself.

And when I found the door was locked,
I pulled and pushed and kicked and knocked.

And when I found the door was shut,
I tried to turn the handle, but –

LEWIS CARROLL
from *Through the Looking-Glass*

Patent No 1

You see, he said, the overall simplicity
Belies the genius that lies beneath.
(Modesty was one of his attributes)
Starting from here, this red liquid
Flows up and down through
Tubes of various sizes, controlling
These, I call them muscles, which
In turn can move these lengths
Of bone, which make the structure.

[208]

There's more to it of course,
But that's the basic stuff.
Then I gave it this skin covering
And tarted the outside up a bit
– I had some time to waste –
It's pleasant to look at, but strictly functional.
I'm really very pleased with it;
I'm going to patent it.
I think I'll call it, 'Trouble'.

KAY HARGREAVES

The Fisherman

The world was first a private park
Until the angel, after dark,
Scattered afar to wests and easts
The lovers and the friendly beasts.

And later still a home-made boat
Contained Creations set afloat,
No rift nor leak that might betray
The creatures to a hostile day.

But now beside the midnight lake
One single fisher sits awake
And casts and fights and hauls to land
A myriad forms upon the sand.

Old Adam on the naming-day
Blessed each and let it slip away:
The fisher of the fallen mind
Sees no occasion to be kind,

[209]

But on his catch proceeds to sup;
Then bends, and at one slurp sucks up
The lake and all that therein is
To slake that hungry gut of his,

Then whistling makes for home and bed
As the last morning breaks in red;
But God the Lord with patient grin
Lets down his hook and hoicks him in.

JAY MACPHERSON

Here and There

There is no place like here
for places on the map
are quite a different sort.

They're neither here nor there
but fixed at where they are;
yet here am I quite caught,

for here cannot be there,
though there is everywhere.
I fly from port to port

since somewhere I must be –
yet nowhere when I'm dead,
and that's a curious thought.

RALPH MEREDITH

Pool

I'm no Alice,
I don't have her curiosity, her stamina;
yet, as I stood at the sink the other night,
I noticed my feet
were in three inches of water.

I looked beyond,
into the dining-room, the hall, the studio –
water was seeping through the carpet
everywhere;
it began to swirl and the house to heave
like a ship afloat.

I didn't taste the water for salt,
I knew it was mainly tears
accumulated under the floorboards
over the years.
Still, I felt confident . . .

Alice, I remembered,
hadn't drowned but floated.

WANDA BARFORD

The Statue

In Parliament Square
there is the statue of a gentleman standing in front of
   a chair.
And all the time that the House of Commons is sitting,
ruling the country, outwitting
each other in the People's name,
some shouting 'Hear, Hear!' and others 'Withdraw' or
   'Shame!'
this distinguished elderly person stands before an empty
   seat,
and every time I pass in the Number 29 bus, I greet
the great man and say with a worried frown:
'Aren't you tired, President Abraham Lincoln?
Why don't you sit down?'

EDITH ROSEVEARE

A Pot Poured Out

A pot poured out
Fulfils its spout

SAMUEL MENASHE

This Our Life

I had the invitation of the King
To go into his House, and, innocent
(Young as I was), I let his servants bring,
And helplessly received, the gifts he sent.
These were they: feet, hands, eyes and right-of-birth;
The clothing and condition of a man;
The strange and ancient liberty of earth.
These I must hold, and use them as I can.
Feet bring fatigue; hands, pain; eyes, too much sight;
Birth, rapture, that declines in doubt and sighing:
The vaunted, vast, and everlasting right
Of living is the liberty of dying.
  'O Lord, have you no other gifts?' I call.
  But he moves silently about his Hall.

HAROLD MONRO

Into My Heart an Air that Kills

Into my heart an air that kills
  From yon far country blows:
What are those blue remembered hills,
  What spires, what farms are those?

That is the land of lost content,
  I see it shining plain,
The happy highways where I went
  And cannot come again.

A. E. HOUSMAN

Going Alone to Spend a Night at the Hsien-Yu Temple

The crane from the shore standing at the top of the steps
The moon on the pool seen at the open door;
Where these are, I made my lodging-place
And for two nights could not turn away.
I am glad I chanced on a place so lonely and still
With no companion to drag me early home.
Now that I have tasted the joy of being alone,
I will never again come with a friend at my side.

PO CHÜ-I
translated by Arthur Waley

To Marguerite

Yes: in the sea of life enisl'd,
With echoing straits between us thrown,
Dotting the shoreless watery wild,
We mortal millions live *alone*.
The islands feel the enclasping flow,
And then their endless bounds they know.

But when the moon their hollows lights
And they are swept by balms of spring,
And in their glens, on starry nights,
The nightingales divinely sing;
And lovely notes, from shore to shore,
Across the sounds and channels pour;

Oh then a longing like despair
Is to their farthest caverns sent;
For surely once, they feel, we were
Parts of a single continent.
Now round us spreads the watery plain –
Oh might our marges meet again!

Who order'd, that their longing's fire
Should be, as soon as kindled, cool'd?
Who renders vain their deep desire? –
A God, a God their severance rul'd;
And bade betwixt their shores to be
The unplumb'd, salt, estranging sea.

MATTHEW ARNOLD

Fragment

I'm happiest when most away
I can bear my soul from its home of clay
On a windy night when the moon is bright
And the eye can wander through worlds of light –

When I am not and none beside –
Nor earth nor sea nor cloudless sky –
But only spirit wandering wide
Through infinite immensity.

EMILY BRONTË

This was one of Emily Brontë's earliest poems.

[215]

On Wenlock Edge

On Wenlock Edge the wood's in trouble;
   His forest fleece the Wrekin heaves;
The gale, it plies the saplings double,
   And thick on Severn snow the leaves.

'Twould blow like this through holt and hanger
   When Uricon the city stood:
'Tis the old wind in the old anger,
   But then it threshed another wood.

Then, 'twas before my time, the Roman
   At yonder heaving hill would stare:
The blood that warms an English yeoman,
   The thoughts that hurt him, they were there.

There, like the wind through woods in riot,
   Through him the gale of life blew high;
The tree of man was never quiet:
   Then 'twas the Roman, now 'tis I.

The gale, it plies the saplings double,
   It blows so hard, 'twill soon be gone:
To-day the Roman and his trouble
   Are ashes under Uricon.

A. E. HOUSMAN

Lights Out

I have come to the borders of sleep,
The unfathomable deep
Forest where all must lose
Their way, however straight,
Or winding, soon or late;
They cannot choose.

Many a road and track
That, since the dawn's first crack,
Up to the forest brink,
Deceived the travellers,
Suddenly now blurs,
And in they sink.

Here love ends,
Despair, ambition ends;
All pleasure and all trouble,
Although most sweet or bitter,
Here ends in sleep that is sweeter
Than tasks most noble.

There is not any book
Or face of dearest look
That I would not turn from now
To go into the unknown
I must enter, and leave, alone,
I know not how.

The tall forest towers;
Its cloudy foliage lowers
Ahead, shelf above shelf;
Its silence I hear and obey
That I may lose my way
And myself.

EDWARD THOMAS

Difficult Relations

Ancient History

Adam, a brown old vulture in the rain,
Shivered below his wind-whipped olive-trees;
Huddling sharp chin on scarred and scraggy knees,
He moaned and mumbled to his darkening brain;
'He was the grandest of them all – was Cain!
'A lion laired in the hills, that none could tire;
'Swift as a stag; a stallion of the plain,
'Hungry and fierce with deeds of huge desire.'

Grimly he thought of Abel, soft and fair –
A lover with disaster in his face,
And scarlet blossom twisted in bright hair.
'Afraid to fight; was murder more disgrace? . . .
'God always hated Cain' . . . He bowed his head –
The gaunt wild man whose lovely sons were dead.

SIEGFRIED SASSOON

My Name and I

The impartial Law enrolled a name
   For my especial use:
My rights in it would rest the same
Whether I puffed it into fame
   Or sank it in abuse.

Robert was what my parents guessed
   When first they peered at me,
And *Graves* an honourable bequest
With Georgian silver and the rest
   From my male ancestry.

They taught me: 'You are *Robert Graves*
   (Which you must learn to spell),
But see that *Robert Graves* behaves,
Whether with honest men or knaves,
   Exemplarily well.'

Then though my I was always I,
   Illegal and unknown,
With nothing to arrest it by –
As will be obvious when I die
   And *Robert Graves* lives on –

I cannot well repudiate
   This noun, this natal star,
This gentlemanly self, this mate
So kindly forced on me by fate,
   Time and the registrar;

And therefore hurry him ahead
   As an ambassador
To fetch me home my beer and bread
Or commandeer the best green bed,
   As he has done before.

[220]

Yet, understand, I am not he
   Either in mind or limb;
My name will take less thought for me,
In worlds of men I cannot see,
   Than ever I for him.

ROBERT GRAVES

`You Live There; I Live Here

. . . You live there; I live here:
Other people everywhere
Haunt their houses, and endure
Days and deeds and furniture,
Circumstances, families,
And the stare of foreign eyes.

Often we must entertain,
Tolerantly if we can,
Ancestors returned again
Trying to be modern man.
Gates of Memory are wide;
All of them can shuffle in,
Join the family, and, once inside,
Alas, what a disturbance they begin!

HAROLD MONRO
from *Strange Meetings*

The Lady and the Gypsy

I handed her my silver
And gullibility,
And tremulously asked her
Who would marry me,
For I was getting older,
Approaching twenty-three –
At least that's what I told her:
All girls, I'm sure, agree
It's sometimes right to suffer
Lapse of memory.

She told me to be patient,
But not for very long,
For down the summer pavement
As lilting as a song
Mr. Right would wander,
Eager, gallant, strong;
And sure enough last summer
My man did come along:
If he is Mr. Right, then
Give me Mr. Wrong.

VERNON SCANNELL

On Jessy Watson's Elopement

Run of is Jessy Watson fair
Her eyes do sparkel, she's good hair.
But Mrs Leath you shal now be
Now and for all Eternity!

MARJORY FLEMING (7)

A fragment from the daily Journals of the most enchanting child writer ever to reach print, the Scottish Marjory Fleming (1803–11), born at Kirkcaldy and dying, perhaps of meningitis, when eight and three-quarters. Set as a task by her much-loved cousin and teacher Isabella, the Journals abound in poems, gossip, rebellious, compassionate and quite original thoughts about everything happening around her. First printed in 1858, they are as vivid and fresh today as when they left her pen.

The Nutcrackers and the Sugar-tongs

The Nutcrackers sate by a plate on the table,
  The Sugar-tongs sate by a plate at his side;
And the Nutcrackers said, 'Don't you wish we were able
  'Along the blue hills and green meadows to ride?
'Must we drag on this stupid existence for ever,
  'So idle and weary, so full of remorse, –
'While every one else takes his pleasure, and never
  'Seems happy unless he is riding a horse?

'Don't you think we could ride without being instructed?
    'Without any saddle, or bridle, or spur?
'Our legs are so long, and so aptly constructed,
    'I'm sure that an accident could not occur.
'Let us all of a sudden hop down from the table,
    'And hustle downstairs, and each jump on a horse!
'Shall we try? Shall we go? Do you think we are able?'
    The Sugar-tongs answered distinctly, 'Of course!'

So down the long staircase they hopped in a minute,
    The Sugar-tongs snapped, and the Crackers said 'crack!'
The stable was open, the horses were in it;
    Each took out a pony, and jumped on his back.
The Cat in a fright scrambled out of the doorway,
    The Mice tumbled out of a bundle of hay,
The brown and white Rats, and the black ones from Norway,
    Screamed out, 'They are taking the horses away!'

The whole of the household was filled with amazement,
    The Cups and the Saucers danced madly about,
The Plates and the Dishes looked out of the casement,
    The Saltcellar stood on his head with a shout,
The Spoons with a clatter looked out of the lattice,
    The Mustard-pot climbed up the Gooseberry Pies,
The Soup-ladle peeped through a heap of Veal Patties,
    And squeaked with a ladle-like scream of suprise.

The Frying-pan said, 'It's an awful delusion!'
    The Tea-kettle hissed and grew black in the face;
And they all rushed downstairs in the wildest confusion,
    To see the great Nutcracker-Sugar-tong race.
And out of the stable, with screamings and laughter,
    (Their ponies were cream-coloured, speckled with brown,)
The Nutcrackers first, and the Sugar-tongs after,
    Rode all round the yard, and then all round the town.

[224]

They rode through the street, and they rode by the station,
    They galloped away to the beautiful shore;
In silence they rode, and 'made no observation',
    Save this: 'We will never go back any more!'
And still you might hear, till they rode out of hearing,
    The Sugar-tongs snap, and the Crackers say 'crack!'
Till far in the distance their forms disappearing,
    They faded away. – And they never came back!

EDWARD LEAR

The Animal House

I have a lion, a furry faced lion.
He dominantly controls the household.
He eats a lot of meat and he snarls if I pester him.
He is out most of the day. I call him dad.

I also have a dove.
She works all day too, but she works at home,
She is soft, gentle, kind and cares for her young,
She is always there if I need her, I call her mum.

I have a peacock.
She has a head with lots of different colours.
She has green eyes and a beautiful coat.
She has a tuft of glittery hair at the front, I call her my punk
    sister.

I have a kitten.
He is so small and smooth.
He has teeny little eyes and a wet nose.
He drinks milk a lot, and cries a lot, I call him baby brother.

Then there's me,
I know what I am.
I'm the black sheep.

SANDY BRECHIN (12)

Paper Matches

My aunts washed dishes while the uncles
squirted each other on the lawn with
    garden hoses. Why are we in here,
I said, and they are out there.
    That's the way it is,
    said Aunt Hetty, the shrivelled-up one.

I have the rages that small animals have,
being small, being animal.
    Written on me was a message,
'At Your Service' like a book of
paper matches. One by one we were
taken out and struck.
    We come bearing supper,
our heads on fire.

PAULETTE JILES

Partly Because

Partly because of the mistakes I made
I felt obliged to say to my son
be kind to people
be a kind seller of seeds
or petrol pump attendant instead of an unkind lawyer
or an uncaring director of personnel.

I could only say it once
and he has gone away
chasing butterflies
but what he does to them
if they are caught
if they are in his power
I am never there to see.

URSULA LAIRD

Ballad of the Dreamy Girl

A pigtail dangled down my back,
I was just sixteen years.
One day my mother came and flicked
a duster round my ears.

'Don't sit there writing poetry,
go dust your room instead!
With all this nonsense you won't earn
the butter on your bread!'

She often scolded me, but I
stepped lightly as a bird
and went on dreaming through the day
as if I had not heard.

What could I say? My mother
would never understand.
So I wrote only secretly,
the duster in my hand.

When finally I learned to cook,
I often heard her tell:
'To keep your future husband sweet,
you'll have to feed him well!'

'And how do men keep women sweet?'
She gave me no reply
but went on cooking, and I saw
her shake her head and sigh.

EDITH ROSEVEARE

Chocolates

Once some people were visiting Chekhov.
While they made remarks about his genius
the Master fidgeted. Finally
he said, 'Do you like chocolates?'

They were astonished, and silent.
He repeated the question,
whereupon one lady plucked up her courage
and murmured shyly, 'Yes.'

'Tell me,' he said, leaning forward,
light glinting from his spectacles,
'what kind? The light, sweet chocolate
or the dark, bitter kind?'

The conversation became general.
They spoke of cherry centres,
of almonds and Brazil nuts.
Losing their inhibitions
they interrupted one another.
For people may not know what they think
about politics in the Balkans,
or the vexed question of men and women,

but everyone has a definite opinion
about the flavour of shredded coconut.
Finally someone spoke of chocolates filled with liqueur,
and everyone, even the author of *Uncle Vanya*,
was at a loss for words.

When they were leaving he stood by the door
and took their hands.
                In the coach returning to Petersburg
they agreed that it had been a most
unusual conversation.

LOUIS SIMPSON

I Know Things

I know things at the side of my head
Like how to fetch the summer home
And how the sands move,
How lustre wanders in mirrors.
But I'm not telling.

I see things at the back of my head
Like where the conversations go
And frosted breath lives,
Where winds gather before they roam.
But I'm not telling. Not ever.

I hear things at the top of my head
Like what sheet music whispers
And what the leaves want,
What letters say before they're a word.
But I'm not telling. Not ever.

Only if you ask!

ADÈLE DAVIDE

On Listening to a Bus Conductor

'Guv!' Means 'Sir!' and 'Luv!'
means 'Madam!' – notes the eager
student from abroad.

ANNE BLOCH

(*Haiku*)

[230]

As It was

It did not seem important at the time:
We gave them pity when they wanted gold,
We could not help it: we were never told.

We'd lost our glasses, so we could not see:
We went home early from the Pantomime –
It did not seem important at the time.

We walked away: it was not our concern.
No doubt there was some fruit upon the Tree:
We'd lost our glasses, so we could not see.

We could not help it: we were never told.
We heard a shot: the guards looked very stern.
We walked away: it was not our concern.

We could not help it: we were never told.
No doubt there were some rumours of a crime,
We'd lost our glasses, so we could not see.
We walked away: it was not our concern.
The streets were dark and it was very cold.
It did not seem important at the time.

JOHN MANDER

Absent Friends

Each writes long letters
to the human being of
thirty years ago.

ANNE BLOCH

(*Haiku*)

[231]

From A Character

With a half-glance upon the sky
At night he said, 'The wanderings
Of this most intricate Universe
Teach me the nothingness of things.'
Yet could not all creation pierce
Beyond the bottom of his eye.

He spake of beauty: that the dull
Saw no divinity in grass,
Life in dead stones, or spirit in air;
Then looking as 'twere in a glass,
He smooth'd his chin and sleek'd his hair,
And said the earth was beautiful.

He spake of virtue: not the gods
More purely, when they wish to charm
Pallas and Juno sitting by:
And with a sweeping of the arm,
And a lack-lustre dead-blue eye,
Devolved his rounded period. . . .

With lips depress'd as he were meek,
Himself unto himself he sold:
Upon himself himself did feed:
Quiet, dispassionate, and cold,
And other than his form of creed,
With chisell'd features clear and sleek.

ALFRED LORD TENNYSON

'Yesterday's Tomorrow, Tomorrow's Yesterday'

Days

What are days for?
Days are where we live.
They come, they wake us
Time and time over.
They are to be happy in:
Where can we live but days?

Ah, solving that question
Brings the priest and the doctor
In their long coats
Running over the fields.

PHILIP LARKIN

Now is Past

Now is past – the happy *now*
  When we together roved
Beneath the wildwood's oak-tree bough
  And nature said we loved.
    Winter's blast
The *now* since then has crept between,
  And left us both apart.
Winters that withered all the green
  Have froze the beating heart.
    Now is past.

Now is past since last we met
  Beneath the hazel bough;
Before the evening sun was set
  Her shadow stretched below.
    Autumn's blast
Has stained and blighted every bough;
  Wild strawberries like her lips
Have left the mosses green below,
  Her bloom's upon the hips.
    Now is past.

Now is past, is changed agen,
  The woods and fields are painted new.
Wild strawberries which both gathered then,
  None know now where they grew.
    The sky's o'ercast,
Wood strawberries faded from wood-sides,
  Green leaves have all turned yellow;
No Adelaide walks the wood-rides,
  True love has no bed-fellow.
    Now is past.

JOHN CLARE

[234]

The Old Man at the Window

'Oh how black the night is,'
said the old man.
'Oh how clear my memories
are.'

The moon is like the
football
I had when I was nine
It bounced three times higher
than any other ball.
Deep down
I am young.
Outside, I'm like metal
Rusting in the rain
Shivering at every wind.

Inside,
I am strong and healthy
Like a full-grown tree.
Outside, I'm old and wrinkled
and feeble
Inside
I am rosy cheeked.

ANTHONY HARVEY (8)

What Did I Lose?

I lost it – what did I lose
In this forest? At midnight I bring a lantern
To stroll in the woods to search;
I recognize the route paved with wild flowers,

Every tree, and every blade of grass. Ah, how did I
Lose it in a place so familiar!
What I lost must be right here, for
Next to this I know no other world.

With a lantern in hand I trace my way step by step.
The dewdrops, glistening, are weeping on the bough.
The stars wink above the trees,
All so quiet, so very quiet, all around.

Really, I did lose it in this place,
With a lantern I have been searching here every night,
But I could not find what I have lost,
Only I know that time hastens me along the path of age.

SUN YÜ-TANG
translated by Kai-yu Hsu

Echo

Walking for the first time
through a strange valley
a murmuring summer afternoon,
I cupped my hands, and shouted,
'Hello. Is anybody there?'

Back came a far-off echo
quivering on the small wind,
sighing among foxgloves and ferns,
'Hello. Is anybody there?'
as if seeking me out.

And returning that mild evening
along the deserted track,
stopped at the same place, and called,
'Hello. Is anybody there?'
but never an answer came,
no matter how many times I spoke;
there was only the hum of late bees
and a donkey braying on the slopes.

Where was echo?
Had it abandoned me?
What had I done to annoy?
Or was there no echo coming that way?

But it was like talking to someone
who does not want to speak,
content to be silent sometimes.

LEONARD CLARK

The Past is Such a Curious Creature

The Past is such a curious Creature
To look her in the Face
A Transport may receipt us
Or a Disgrace –

Unarmed if any meet her
I charge him fly
Her faded Ammunition
Might yet reply.

EMILY DICKINSON

Creatures of Early Morning

Creatures of early morning,
The catchers-up with homework,
The busy tolerant birds, and
The tiptoe makers of tea,
Allies, conspirators,
Privileged travellers,
Guests in this clear country
(Never to be stayed in,
Each time to be discovered)
Where even the rain is private –
A personal matter between us –
Who knows the taste of the hour
Better than we?

Yesterday's tomorrow,
Tomorrow's yesterday,
Today waits for its story.
Whatever is told, will stay.

NAOMI LEWIS

The Road

There is a road that turning always
   Cuts off the country of Again.
Archers stand there on every side
   And as it runs Time's deer is slain,
   And lies where it has lain.

That busy clock shows never an hour.
   All flies and all in flight must tarry.
The hunter shoots the empty air
   Far on before the quarry,
   Which falls though nothing's there to parry.

The lion couching in the centre
   With mountain head and sunset brow
Rolls down the everlasting slope
   Bones picked an age ago,
   And the bones rise up and go.

There the beginning finds the end
   Before beginning ever can be,
And the great runner never leaves
   The starting and the finishing tree,
   The budding and the fading tree.

There the ship sailing safe in harbour
   Long since in many a sea was drowned.
The treasure burning in her hold
   So near will never be found,
   Sunk past all sound.

There a man on a summer evening
  Reclines at ease upon his tomb
And is his mortal effigy.
  And there within the womb,
  The cell of doom,

The ancestral deed is thought and done,
  And in a million Edens fall
A million Adams drowned in darkness
  For small is great and great is small,
  And a blind seed all.

EDWIN MUIR

During Wind and Rain

They sing their dearest songs –
He, she, all of them – yea,
Treble and tenor and bass,
  And one to play;
With the candles mooning each face. . . .
  Ah, no; the years O!
How the sick leaves reel down in throngs!

They clear the creeping moss –
Elders and juniors – aye,
Making the pathways neat
  And the garden gay;
And they build a shady seat. . . .
  Ah, no; the years, the years;
See, the white storm-birds wing across!

[240]

They are blithely breakfasting all –
Men and maidens – yea,
Under the summer tree,
  With a glimpse of the bay,
While pet fowl come to the knee. . . .
   Ah, no; the years O!
And the rotten rose is ript from the wall.

They change to a high new house,
He, she, all of them – aye,
Clocks and carpets and chairs
  On the lawn all day,
And brightest things that are theirs. . . .
   Ah, no; the years, the years;
Down their carved names the rain-drop ploughs.

THOMAS HARDY

Parting

The Past is a strange land, most strange.
Wind blows not there, nor does rain fall:
If they do, they cannot hurt at all.
Men of all kinds as equals range

The soundless fields and streets of it.
Pleasure and pain there have no sting,
The perished self not suffering
That lacks all blood and nerve and wit,

And is in shadow-land a shade.
Remembered joy and misery
Bring joy to the joyous equally;
Both sadden the sad. So memory made

Parting to-day a double pain:
First because it was parting; next
Because the ill it ended vexed
And mocked me from the Past again,

Not as what had been remedied
Had I gone on, – not that, oh no!
But as itself no longer woe;
Sighs, angry word and look and deed

Being faded: rather a kind of bliss,
For there spiritualized it lay
In the perpetual yesterday
That naught can stir or strain like this.

EDWARD THOMAS

Lament of a Slug-a-bed's Wife

Get up thou lazy lump thou log get up
For it is very nearly time to sup
And did the Saviour die that thou should'st be
In bed for breakfast, dinner, lunch and tea?

STEVIE SMITH

Six Things for Christmas

I wish to be given beautiful things this Christmas,
Beautiful but impossible
For gifts that are fresh are nice
But the joy is soon gone
And only the physical volume remains
To be pleasantly taken for granted.
But if an object is lost
Then a small pain is born
And goes in search, beseeching,
To embrace the thing that was.
And should the thing be regiven
Then embraced with that small pain
It becomes a thing of beauty.

So, six things that once upon a time
I lost:
One: is a bald sad man I lost somewhere
Within my seventeenth year.
Two: was an acquaintance that I had with Mt. Kerinyaga,
Whom I also loved.
Three: a parcel of thoughts that I continually lose.
Four: a mouse called Nuisance that was all grey.
Five: a beautiful Aunt who gave me a sight
Of two grey heron when I was a boy.
Six: that thing we all lost so long ago – Christmas.

JOHN MAY

Acknowledgements

The editor gratefully acknowledges permission to use the following copyright material:

'Poems of Solitary Delights' (Tachibana Akemi) and 'Lullabies' (Anon) from *The Penguin Book of Japanese Verse*, trans. Geoffrey Bownas and Anthony Thwaite (The Penguin Poets 1964) pp. 142–3, 144, Copyright © Geoffrey Bownas and Anthony Thwaite, 1964; '*Kinder-und Hausmärchen*' by Brian Alderson from *The Brothers Grimm: Popular Folk Tales*, published by Victor Gollancz Ltd, © Brian Alderson, 1978; an extract from 'In Memory of W. B. Yeats' reprinted by permission of Faber and Faber Ltd from *The English Auden* by W. H. Auden; 'Conversation with an Angel' and 'Pool' by Wanda Barford, by permission of the author; 'Café' by Hala Baykov, by permission of the author; 'On Listening to a Bus Conductor', 'Absent Friends', 'My Dreams are Lucid' and '*Pied à Terre*' by Anne Bloch, by permission of the author; 'The Animal House' by Sandy Brechin, award-winner in the 1982 W. H. Smith Young Writers Competition and first published in *Young Writers*, 24th Year (Heinemann Educational Books); 'By St Thomas Water' from *Collected Poems* by Charles Causley, published by Macmillan; 'The First Step' by C. P. Cavafy, translated by Edmund Keeley and Philip Sherrard, from *The Collected Poems*, reprinted by permission of Chatto & Windus; 'Echo' and 'Parakeet' from *The Corn Growing* by Leonard Clark, published by Hodder and Stoughton; 'Monkeys' from *Poems* by Padraic Colum, published by Macmillan Publishing Company New York, by permission of the Estate of Padraic Colum and the administrators of the Estate of Emmet Greene; 'So They Went Deeper into the Forest' and 'Noah' from *The Chequered Shade* by Roy Daniells, used by permission of The Canadian Publishers McClelland and Stewart Limited, Toronto; 'My Youngest Daughter' and 'I Know Things' by Adèle Davide, by permission of the author; an extract from 'The Children of Stare', 'Peak and Puke', 'Tom's Angel', by Walter de la Mare, reprinted by permission of the Literary Trustees of Walter de la Mare and the Society of Authors as their representative; 'The Wind Tapped like a Tired Man', 'A Bird Came Down the Walk', 'Because I Could not Stop for Death', 'The Past is such a Curious Creature' by Emily

[245]

[247]

Tabitha Tuckett, award-winner in the 1982 W. H. Smith Young Writers Competition and first published in *Young Writers*, 24th Year (Heinemann Educational Books); 'Where Do Old Things Go to' by Arthur Waley, reprinted by permission of Mrs Alison Waley; Three poems from *Chinese Poems* translated by Arthur Waley, reprinted by permission of George Allen & Unwin; 'A Form of Epitaph' from *Audible Silence* by Lawrence Whistler, reprinted by permission of the author; 'The First Thing to Do in a House' by Anna Wickham, reprinted by permission of James Hepburn; and 'The Boy at the Window', reprinted by permission of Faber and Faber Ltd from *Poems 1943–56* by Richard Wilbur.

Acknowledgements are also made to the few copyright-holders whom the editor has been unable to trace in spite of careful enquiry.

Index of Authors

Index of First Lines

[253]

[254]